HARNESS YOUR PURPOSE, POWER AND PEACE.

Discover the Leader Within You

GINA YARRISH

Table of Contents

Introduction 5

Chapter 1 Creating Results 7

Chapter 2 Imagination 28

Chapter 3 Value of Specificity.. 48

Chapter 4 Your Decisions Have Weight............................ 60

Chapter 5 Obstacles You Will Face 70

Chapter 6 Trusting the Process and Leaving Worry Behind 78

Chapter 7 Being Open to Outcome, Not How 86

Chapter 8 Focus with Results 101

Chapter 9 Perception.. 115

Chapter 10 The Frequency of Your Thoughts................. 127

Chapter 11 Become a Magnet: Put on the Becoming.................. 139

Chapter 12 Gratitude and Support................................. 149

About the Author... 162

To my husband, who is forever supportive of what I'm doing with never ending love and to my children Michael and Melissa who are forever at my side, assisting in growing and learning with me. With all my heart and love. Thank you!

Introduction

Is it possible to take hold of your life and create the situations and results you want? I think so. In fact, one question that I've learned to frequently ask myself is "Am I living by default, or by design?" In other words, am I allowing life to simply happen, or am I actively planning it? I think it's possible to take charge of your destiny and create the life you want to lead.

That's why I'm writing this book. I want you to think that the above is possible too. In fact, I want you to truly believe that you have the ability to change your life and create your own destiny. By the time you finish reading this book, you're going to fully understand why I *know* that all you need to do is follow a few basic principles to see incredible results.

These are principles that you can apply to every area of your life. As you move through the book, I want you to think about these areas—your career, relationships, health, finances, and freedom, for example—and imagine how you can revolutionize the way you think about them. Remember that this is your life, and there isn't anything more important; planning is imperative. We can't get to where we want to go without first thinking it.

Stop waiting around for your dreams to drop into your lap! Have faith in your ability, recognize that you deserve the best, and learn how to create the results you want.

Chapter 1

Creating Results

Everything is created twice, first in thought
then in reality.
—Robin Sharma

Creating results is fun! I mean, it should be fun when we are doing what we love and working towards what we long for, right? If you haven't taken the time to plan out your life before, this may be a little challenging. Don't let this discourage you! Remember that when we're challenged, we're growing—and nobody said that it was going to be easy. Creating the results we want is going to take time, consistency, and determination. This doesn't mean that you should give up. Don't accept less just because you're worried! Be positive and go for what you really want. Yes, at times it will be difficult and challenging, but the gains are enormous and worth every ounce of effort.

CHANGE IS GOOD, COMFORT IS NOT

The thing to keep in mind is that, at heart, we are creatures of habit. We crave the kind of comfort that repetition brings, even if that repetition is ultimately holding us back. We tend to think that being uncomfortable is a bad thing and even avoid situations that make us unsure of ourselves. Unfortunately, comfort doesn't necessarily promote growth. Over the years, I've learned that if we really want to live life to its fullest, then we have to know that being uncomfortable is our best friend. We are never growing, learning, and moving up the ladder of life, in other words, if we are always comfortable.

What does being uncomfortable feel like? You all know the sensation—and for some, as soon as it shows up, you literally step back or make no advancing moment. Let me give you an example. Let's pretend that you're thinking about joining a new club or organization of some sort. It will be fun, you think, and you'll meet some new people, possibly network for some new business, and maybe help the community in the process. Exciting!

Joining this club is something you've always wanted to do … but then you start to "self-talk," and the doubts roll in. *You have no time for the club—and even if you did, they probably wouldn't like you anyway, so what's the point? You don't know what you were thinking, considering adding something else to your already impossible schedule. And what will your friends and family think? It's probably just a waste of time.*

Does any of the above sound familiar? I bet that it does. It certainly sounds familiar to me, at least. Let me give you another scenario. You want to go to the club meeting, and it doesn't really matter what anyone else thinks. You could easily make time in your schedule, yet it doesn't happen. In both cases, why do you think that is? Why are you unable to commit to something new?

Because you're living life by default instead of creating what you want. You're either talking yourself out of the new experience, or you're just not making the commitment to do it because it's easier to keep doing what you've always done. In order to do what you want, you have to do the things that seem risky, or uncomfortable, in order to create the results you want.

Are there going to be challenges? Will there be some uncomfortableness? Of course! But would you rather have a life you love living and creating, or one that is just happening around you?

CREATING RESULTS

Now that you understand why being uncomfortable and embracing change is a good thing, you will better understand how to create results.

Creating results requires us to think about what we want out of life. Whether or not it's immediately apparent, most of us have some amazing talents already. We can use these to help create the results we want! The only reason they haven't already helped us achieve our goals is that we tend to have detrimental habits and patterns. Whenever I was uncomfortable, for example, I would procrastinate and put off things that needed to be done. I knew I could do them better, but the thought of failing held me back until the very last moment. Sometimes I would go way overboard due to my perfectionism. Probably the most commonly demonstrated habit—that I practically made a career out of—was that of an "excuse-aholic." I would be so busy doing other things and creating excuses that I just never seemed to get around to what I knew I really wanted to do. Why? Most likely because even though I knew I

9

wanted it, I would have had to change and be uncomfortable in the process.

These are just a few of the things that hold us back from creating the life for which we long. Think about it. If we didn't have excuses—and I mean *none*—how would life be different?

If we didn't procrastinate, what would be different right now? Your house would be cleaner, you job would be paying you more, and your relationships would be more loving and caring because you would have committed the time, effort, and change required to really help them develop. If none of those things are true, then you should start considering that maybe there are some things about yourself that you need to change.

Great news: you can change whatever you don't want.
You CAN change!

LIVE LIFE BY DESIGN

Let me share a story about a client of mine, Barbara. Barbara was a stay-at-home mom, a supportive wife, and a loving daughter. She has many responsibilities. Mothers out there, you know what it's like to run a house with children, and what a day looks like— filled with cooking, cleaning, sports, laundry, homework, caring for parents and children, visits to the doctors, and having dinner on the table when the hubby comes home. But wait, because her day wasn't over. She also had to schedule the dentist appointment, arrange for a carpool, and did I mention that she longs for more?

Barbara is a great example of what it looks like to procrastinate under the guise of legitimate concerns. Her limiting beliefs and excuses were that she had to be home for the kids. She had to take care of her parents. She had to be at every game and be sure to put everyone else first. And to be fair, she had a great life. She wasn't complaining about it at all. But what she discovered was that she could be and do so much more. She could do what she loved and still have everything else in her life—she wasn't losing anything by pursuing more. Was she happier when she figured this out? Yes!

Are you wondering what Barbara had to do in order to start living life by design? Once again, we have to consider what exactly we want from life. What is our life purpose? What will bring us happiness and joy? For Barbara, she realized that she wanted a career. She loved being a mother, wife, and daughter, but she also wanted a career of her own outside of the home.

What did that realization mean for Barbara? Well, the same thing that we've been discussing all along. She began to worry about change, and the sense of discomfort came creeping in. She wondered if she had the knowledge and know-how to do what she wanted. Would she be successful? How would the family take it? Would they be okay with a schedule change and mom not always being here?

Do you see a pattern here? The worries that Barbara had are the same worries that we had in our hypothetical situation of joining a new club! If we allow our thoughts to wander, we move away from what we want while just allowing things to happen. The results that we end up with reflect that decision to just passively let life pass us by. We are more afraid of what we are thinking and feeling than we are about the potential gain. It takes ten seconds to walk in the door. It takes five seconds to say "hi" to someone. You get my point, right? We spend way too much time in our thoughts, and those thoughts bring results we don't want. We need to stay focused on the thoughts we *do* want. Don't worry about feeling nervous—we all do. Just walk forward. Lean in.

Believe me, I understand how hard that advice can be. Let's talk about my own personal brand of anxiety-induced avoidance. I call it my "self-talk," which directly influences my thoughts and, therefore, my actions. It can keep me from going through the doors that help create my self-image, and eventually lead to my reaction. These results impact my behavior, which adds gas to the engine and brings us back to my "self-talk." This pattern is what gave me the results I had. *How we do one thing is how we do everything.* Learning to change one habit can have an amazing result and completely change our lives.

Think about being comfortable as the same thing as a thermostat. Our comfort is staying in the zone. Whenever we get close to the room temperature, we stop moving forward. If whatever we're about to experience is outside of that temperature range, we subconsciously hold ourselves back. Our bodies send out a mental signal—tension—and we stop. We unconsciously pull away and step back. As a result, we subconsciously create a reality that matches our self-image and mindset.

How can you change this pattern? Start getting the results you want. Jack Canfield has an exercise that you would love.

E + R = O

Jack Canfield and the theory behind E + R = 0; event plus response equals outcome. If you want to change the outcome, you first have to know what outcome it is you want. How do we do this? Well, we start with our thoughts. You can already see how thoughts change response. Thoughts are an emotion, an extension of how we feel. If we don't like how we feel, we need to change the thought and the outcome will be different. Our mind is the most powerful part of our body. It is the center of our life and dictates how we feel, what we do, and when we do it. Should we not feed it goodness, love it, and care for it with positive habits and patterns?

Of course we should! Let's start thinking about how we can change our thought patterns to get the results we want. Here are some great ways to help channel negative emotions and change the way we think and feel in order to change our lives.

A. Hit the pause button just like on the remote control of the television. Pause the thought and change the channel. You do it all the time in real life, so why not mentally?

B. Change a (channel) negative thought immediately into the opposite.

Negative Thought	Change the Channel
I never get what I want.	Everything I desire comes to me willingly.
There is no money here to be made.	Money comes to me easily and in abundance.
I will never lose weight.	Weight comes off freely as I eat healthy food.

What you think affects the results you are getting.

Changing the thoughts changes the results.

C. Get into the practice of leaving words such as *not, can't, won't, shouldn't,* and *don't* out of your vocabulary. These are words that hold you back from creating what you want.

D. Get rid of negative actions and behaviors. STOP doing what doesn't give you what you want!

- Stop complaining about what you don't have or what someone has done.
- Stop feeling sorry for yourself because you're not skinny.
- Stop sitting on the couch, complaining about how dirty the house is.

If you're going to change the pattern, you have to replace it with another action or thought that better supports the outcome for which you're looking. Let me give you an example.

Let's pretend someone is talking badly about you. Complaining about this will get you nowhere, but it *does* kill time as well as create more aggravation, stress, and anxiety for yourself. The solution? Let them talk. It's probably not true anyway, or they don't have the full story. What do you think this negative person wants to do? Pull you down with them, of course. If you talk and complain about the situation, then you're giving them those results while also ensuring that you get negative results yourself in the form of more negative talk, frustration, stress, and anxiety. Is that what you want?

PICK YOUR BATTLES

There is that old saying to "pick your battles." I sure as heck would much rather pick battles that will give me more love, happiness, and wealth rather than frustration and negativity.

Okay, let's talk about how you replace old behavior with new behavior that will get you better results and outcomes. Here are a few examples that can help you.

- Feeling sorry for yourself because of your weight?
    1. Eat smaller portions.
    2. Eat less junk.
    3. Join a group that walks.

Instead of just complaining with no plan of action, take those negative feelings and thoughts and channel them into a tangible plan. There are three actions steps up there, and I suggest you write them down, set a goal (results) you want, and then think about how you will know you've reached it. Having measurable goals is important. For example, saying something like "I will know I reached my goal when I weight 160" is more productive than just saying "I'll know I've reached my goal when I'm thinner."

Remember what Jack says about E + O = R. What is the emotion and outcome? **E**motion is *lazy* + **O**utcome is *sitting on the couch*, which equals the **R**esults of an *unclean house*. Is that the kind of way you want to live? Let's take that example and look at some actions you can take.

Action steps to take:

Get rid of negative thoughts like "I don't have the motivation to clean." Change the thought to "I am motivated, and I love when my house smells and looks clean."

Replace the inaction with action: you either do it yourself, ask a friend to help, or hire someone to help you. The end results are what? Let's go back to the equation:

$$E + R = O$$

Emotion: (Thought: I can do this with or without help.)

Result: Cleaning the house

Outcome: The house is cleaned, looks amazing, and smells good.

Here's an interesting thought: how we do one thing is how we do everything. If your house is not clean, what does your car, work place, garage, or barn look like? When you create results in one area, other areas will begin to improve as well.

ARE YOU READY TO GET COMMITTED TO YOU?

Creating results will take commitment and an investment in yourself. This doesn't mean just doing it once or twice. To change old patterns and habits, you have to get some motivation and support to keep up the change until the subconscious mind just does it instinctively. This is kind of like brushing your teeth. You don't really think about it—it's just something you do. You don't think about having negative thoughts—you just do it. These are all things you have been taught over time. We are influenced by parents, grandparents, friends, siblings, priests, pastors, teachers, and bosses. Anyone that is in your life will have an influence on you—it's up to you to determine whether or not you take that influence to heart and allow it to take over your life.

These are patterns and habits we have learned over time, especially when we were children. We did what our parents did or what they showed us. If you were the child and they were the adults, then you learned from them. Now think about how you might be influencing others. Is it good/positive? Is it bad/negative?

THE POWER OF COMMITMENT

I remember when commitment was the biggest challenge for me. It might be the same thing for you too. It's so easy to do things the way they have always been done rather than to put effort into changing them. But I assure you that the time, effort, and determination is all worth it. Let's take a look at someone who did just that.

I recently had a woman named Kim reach out to me. She was depressed, out of work, tired of getting help from others, had put on a huge amount of weight, and was essentially in crisis mode. Life was not at all what she thought it would be. Kim wanted to do so much more. So we talked about what she wanted.

The conversation started with Kim's current situation and why she thought she'd ended up there. Then we discussed what it was she truly wanted. Her focus was on what she didn't have and wasn't getting. We know thoughts lead to results, right? So we had to change her thoughts. Instead of what she didn't have, I asked her what she would love to do.

She said that she'd love a job working with elderly. As soon as Kim changed her focus, I could hear the excitement in her voice. She described what she wanted and why she wanted it, and it turned out she wanted to help the elderly because of her own experience with being in a wheelchair and what she had to do to overcome it. She knew that she could help others and wanted to do so.

I asked her what else she would love. She said that she'd love to not be so depressed and overweight. She'd love to have a relationship with someone that would love her for who she was, and she'd love to be more active and go for long walks. Again, you could hear something in her voice come to life. It was great!

17

What we see is where we are right now. Between where we are and where we want to be is perceived as a gap. This gap could be like stormy waters sometimes and other times as calm as could be. Some may look at it and say there is no way to get from here to there. This is because we cannot possibly see every step we have to take to get the results—it simply looks impossible. So we stay where we are getting the same results, regardless of whether we actually want them or not.

Not for Kim, however—not any longer. Our conversation carried on like this: If you could have a relationship, what would it look like? If you had the career of which you dream, where would it be and with whom? What would you be doing? If you want to lose weight, how much would you like to weigh?

We created an action plan for Kim. What could she do with what she had? She looked into different jobs, she decided to join a local club to meet some new friends, and she decided that she would walk to the store so she would get some exercise. All in all, her plan was a great start to being uncomfortable (and working towards change!).

Several weeks passed, and she did everything she had on her action plan. With delight and joy, she reached out to me once more. She shared that she met an amazing man named Brian. He was everything she wanted. She also applied for several jobs and got the one she wanted. Oh, man! It was awesome stuff, and today as I write this she tells me she just registered for a 5K run. Oh my goodness! When you plan for the results you want, do you see what begins to happen?

What areas of your life do you want to start planning? Do you want a healthier, more loving and intimate relationship with your husband? Perhaps a supportive relationship with your boss? Maybe a stronger friendship with your kids? Or maybe you'd rather start planning for the job you long for but never went after. How would life be different?

What are you waiting for? Forget being uncomfortable! The end results are powerful with an emotional upward pull to a freer, fuller life like you've never experienced before.

HORSES AND HUMANS

Now, how does this idea of commitment and planning for the life you want show up with horses and humans? Think about living by default. In this situation, your goal is to go down to the barn and take your partner out for a ride, or perhaps work with some obstacles in the arena. There is no set intention for what it is you want. This could go well, or it could be really bad and ugly.

Let me give you an example. We venture down to the barn, partner up with one of the horses, and head out to the pasture to play on the ground with some obstacles. When we get out there, the horse is indecisive about going over the jumps or going through the car wash. Why do you think that is? I've asked for some circles, and all I get is wonky ovals. Have I created a plan for success or created the results I wanted? Not at all. In this instance, I just figuratively walked through life allowing things to be and happen as they happened. It's no wonder I didn't get the results I was searching, right?

Creating the results takes planning. What does that mean for your everyday life? Well, let's talk about what a typical day full of mindful planning might look like. Let's say that today is 'relationships day.' How could I build a stronger relationship with my horse that would reflect in everything I do as a person? I would go into the barn, take my time to comb and brush him up, then go

19

for a walk in the green grass and let him eat some fresh clippings. Then I'd head off to the pasture to play. I would like ten circles at trot and five at walk. I'd reward my horse with a treat, then move on to the sidewalks along the fence for twenty feet to the jumps. I'd like five jumps without hesitation. I'd reward the horse with some rubbing and then allow him to graze in the field before the trip back up to the barn. How do you think our relationship would improve?

CREATE YOUR REALITY

What if I were talking about a client rather than a horse? Maybe my client isn't sure what career she wants. When she comes into the arena, her task is to pick three careers that she would love and set those objects in the arena. Next she would have to walk around the objects to discuss the benefit of each job while the horse is at liberty (no rope). If she is in alignment with what she wants and has created it in her mind, the horse will be willing go with her. If she isn't in alignment, he will be unclear and she'll get caught up in "fix mode" while losing focus about what she would love.

Where does this kind of situation show up for you?

Clear thoughts, positive energy, and planning all come with a healthy mind. What can one do to improve this? We just spoke about negative behaviors and creating the results we want with planning. What I didn't mention was that in the process of changing, there can be some areas of stress and a lack of clarity. If you know my story, then you know that stress was my sister. I was the master at creating it. In order to change this, I knew I needed to change more than just my thoughts.

You see, creating sustainable results is a form of inward healing. Not only was I healing my mind, I was also healing the internal parts of my body. I was working on creating the results I wanted in order to allow my insides to match my outsides. Many that come to see me at the farm are working on this same process. Taking the time to work on me brought me into alignment, and now I can live a free, full, and healthy life while achieving the results for which I longed.

I didn't do all of this on my own. I knew that I needed additional support with the inward healing that was happening to me. This is when I discovered essential oils. I am not one for medicine, so when I discovered the power of essential oils, I had to know more. Plus, they're all natural!

Today I use only essential oils. Young Living Essential Oils, that is. YL makes some amazing oils that help heal from the inside out too—just like creating happiness comes from the inside out. My lifesaver was one called "Stress Away." I would put it in my water several times a day. Thank goodness you cannot overdose because my body surely needed it. You use as often as necessary, and over time you will see that you are using it less and less. Don't be afraid to learn a new way to deal with negative emotions and thoughts. Don't be afraid to be uncomfortable. Essential oils are a part of my daily diet and well-being. I don't know where I would be without them. Other oils I often use are "Magnify Your Purpose" and "Hope." These specific oils help me with grounding and clarity.

If you want more details on the oils, then I encourage you to go to Young Living Essential Oils at www.GinaYarrish.com/EO

You may be wondering if we use the oils on our horses, and the answer is yes. They can be used for horses, dogs, cats, family members, friends, and clients.

When we heal from the inside out, it is sustainable and measurable. Here I am writing a book. Before creating success, I never could have dreamed of creating something like this.

Today, I know the power behind creating an amazing life, and I wouldn't give my horses, my oils, or my passion for helping others up for anything. Going back, NO WAY! Forward and upward. Lean in and focus forward.

To help you along your journey, I will mention specific Young Living Essential Oil Brand oils throughout the book. I've also created worksheet activities that will help you Harness your Purpose, Power, and Peace. God Bless and enjoy the journey.

To get you started and sharing with your horses or pets, try some of these:

A fulfilled life starts with grounding yourself mentally, emotionally, and spiritually. A great choice for that is **Galbanum™** essential oil. It has many uses, but its fragrance influences harmony and balance as well as amplifying spiritual awareness and meditation.

Grounding™ is a balancing blend of scents used for feelings of clarity or to enhance spirituality.

For more information about oils, please visit my website at www.ginayarrish.com/EO.

Creating Results Activity

What would you love? What do you long to create? What would really excite you and light your fire?

Relationships _____

_____

_____

Career _____

_____

_____

Wealth _____

_____

_____

Health _____

_____

_____

Freedom _____

_____

_____

What negative behaviors do you have to let go of?

_____

_____

_____

What will you replace them with?

_____
_____
_____

What is the outcome you honestly want?

_____
_____
_____

How will you know when you've reached your goal (measurable results)?

_____
_____
_____

Who can support you on your journey (friend, pastor, sibling, mentor, coach)?

_____
_____
_____
_____

How will you stay committed?_____

_____
_____
_____
_____
_____

Gina Yarrish

Chapter 2

Imagination

What the mind can conceive and believe, it can achieve.

—Napoleon Hill, author of *Think and Grow Rich*

As children, we dream about what life could be. We use our imaginations. As a young girl, I remember playing house. I'd put on my apron, push the chair up to the counter, and get all the ingredients out to start baking cookies. I was using my imagination to create something in the future. Those where the days, when I used my child-sized vacuum and went around the house cleaning. I would even talk to myself as if I were the woman of the house. Can you relate to this as a child?

For me, imagination didn't end there. Later in the day, I would set up my blackboard and all my stuffed animals around the room to sit in my classroom. You see, I was going to be a teacher. Reflecting back, I didn't know what kind of teacher, but I would be helping others. Everything we do prepares us for what's to come.

What did you do growing up? Were you the person who wanted to be a singer? I remember my sister using a hairbrush, maybe a spoon—anything that was in the shape of a microphone, really—to start singing into. She does sing pretty well.

If you can take yourself back to that time and place, how did it make you feel? I bet you weren't thinking of anything else, not a care in the world. You were focused on doing exactly what you wanted to do and on making the world exactly what you wanted it to be.

LOSS OF IMAGINATION

Somewhere along the line, we lose this laser focus and life gets serious. We forget about using one of the many mental faculties we have, mostly because we were never taught how to use it. If your parents were like mine, at some point in growing up, it was all about getting serious and stopping those silly things. So what did we do? We listened and got serious. Why do you think that is?

PURPOSE IN LIFE

Honestly, I think it's mostly because of human lack of understanding. We all have a purpose here in life—a life that continues to move forward whether we want it to or not. There is this thing called time, which is but an illusion but never stops. We can stand still, but for us it will either be pulling us down or pulling us up. Learning shouldn't stop when we get out of high school or college. We should be forever growing. The whole purpose of our time here on earth is to grow and expand. Life should be amazing—not full of static and stagnancy. Granted, our choices in life produce the results we get. Are you one of those people who refuses to grow and learn and must do things your way? Let me ask you, "How is that working out for you?"

OVERCOME LIFE'S CROSSROADS

There are so many crossroads in life that are, to be honest, very scary. But we can't get to what where truly want if we first don't imagine it. For the billions of people in the world who are very successful, do you think they aren't scared? We have this crazy image that they can't be scared in order to have that success. It's just the opposite for so many. What I have come to realize is that being scared only lasts a few seconds. But our mind blows everything out of proportion. For some, their obstacle looks really huge and it feels like the world is going to end; for others, it looks like a complete meltdown with evidence of anxiety all over their faces. This simply should not be. We need to rein in our reactions and get control of what we are thinking, just like we rein in kids so they don't get wild.

Let's use this metaphor: if you're at a crossroad and not sure what to do, think of this. Whatever fear you face, it isn't really as scary as the image you are creating that makes it scary. The important thing is to take a step forward. That crossroad could feel like you're on the edge of a cliff. What if you changed that image and you look again? Turns out it wasn't a cliff, but just a curb. Could you take a step then? Of course. Rein it in and remind yourself to imagine what you want, not what you don't want.

VIBRATION THAT ATTRACTS MORE

Let me take you back to my childhood and share what happened when I used my imagination. There is something about imagination that brings it to life. It is the feeling of fun and excitement around what it is we want to do. When I was play cooking, I was excited; with excitement comes an increased heart rate that sends out positive vibrations to the universe. Along with these positive vibrations comes positive results. What we think and how we respond give us the direct results. This is not a new idea. This concept has been around for thousands of years. It is just now you are hearing it.

This is powerful stuff when you learn to tap into it. That is tapping into YOU. How you think, what you think, when you think, and what you're thinking about matters. Harnessing success is about *you*.

STRUGGLES ALONG THE WAY

We all struggle with life, and not everyone will agree with what you're doing or thinking. I can recall some who may not have liked what I was doing or how I was playing. From young to old, there are people out there that would tell me to "stop that silliness." They thought that it was time to get real and think about "important" things. What happens when we're confronted with these people? Unfortunately, these negative interactions can influence our daily habits and routines and, ultimately, mold what we believe about ourselves.

You see, life is made up of patterns and habits. The pattern here creates a shift in the outcome that will change your life until you see otherwise. These patterns and habits are known as our belief system, and our belief system plays an important part in our life. In this instance, we will stop playing for a time period, until the person who disapproves is gone. Then we might go right back to playing—until they come back, that is. The person in question might be a parent, a friend, or a sibling—anyone who is in your life could potentially fill this role.

I've mentioned this saying before: how we do one thing is how we do everything. It's true in this situation too. Let's keep in mind the example of a small child's imagination versus the "real world" mentality of friends or family. Picture a small child just beginning to discover the world and hungry to learn. We see a passion for imagination and playing. Then someone comes along and tells her to grow up. In the same way, when someone comes in and shuts us down, an incongruence begins to form in our belief system. Our insides say "yes!" to imagination and exploration, but the external part—the part that has to fit in with society and follow rules—says "NO!"

We tell ourselves that playing is silly and that we shouldn't do it. Are you beginning to see this in other areas of life? Maybe when cleaning your room, for example, where you feel like you've done your best but someone else tells you that, no, that's not what a clean room looks like. Or maybe you'd like to dress a certain way and someone says that it's not appropriate. Do you see the pattern now? We fall into a habit of creating not the person we want to be, but rather the person that other people want. Externally we are trying to do what others want us to do, in other words, and the thinking pattern tends to place more importance on what others want from us instead of what *we* want from us. In fact, this pattern can go so deep for so long that we end up having no real idea of what we want.

If that is you, no worries. You're in a great place, reading a great book that will help you to lean in and get forward momentum.

Some may call those that won't allow someone to be

themselves a dream stealer. Let me share an amazing story of a dream stealer and talk about why it's so important to go with what you believe in, long for, and desire.

"THE HORSE RANCH STORY"

Hold onto your dreams, regardless of what anyone else says. I recently heard a true story, told by Jack Canfield, about a boy who used his imagination to create a dream:

I have a friend named Monty Roberts who owns a horse ranch in San Ysidro. He has let me use his house to put on fundraising events to raise money for youth-at-risk programs. The last time I was there, he introduced me by saying, "I want to tell you why I let Jack use my house. It all goes back to a story about a young man who was the son of an itinerant horse trainer who would go from stable to stable, race track to race track, farm to farm, and ranch to ranch, training horses. As a result, the boy's high school career was continually interrupted. When he was a senior, he was asked to write a paper about what he wanted to be and do when he grew up.

"That night, he wrote a seven-page paper describing his goal of someday owning a horse ranch. He wrote about his dream in great detail, and he even drew a diagram of a 200-acre ranch, showing the location of all the buildings, the stables, and the track. Then he drew a detailed floor plan for a 4,000-square-foot house that would sit on a 200-acre dream ranch.

"He put a great deal of his heart into the project, and the next day he handed it in to his teacher. Two days later he received his paper back. On the front page was a large red F with a note that read, 'See me after class.'

"The boy with the dream went to see the teacher after class

and asked, 'Why did I receive an F?' The teacher said, 'This is an unrealistic dream for a young boy like you. You have no money. You come from an itinerant family. You have no resources. Owning a horse ranch requires a lot of money. You have to buy the land. You have to pay for the original breeding stock, and later you'll have to pay large stud fees. There's no way you could ever do it.' Then the teacher added, 'If you will rewrite this paper with a more realistic goal, I will reconsider your grade.'

"The boy went home and thought about it long and hard. He asked his father what he should do. His father said, 'Look, son, you have to make up your own mind on this. However, I think it is a very important decision for you.' Finally, after sitting with it for a week, the boy turned in the same paper, making no changes at all. He stated, 'You can keep the F and I'll keep my dream.'"

Monty then turned to the assembled group and said, "I tell you this story because you are sitting in my 4,000-square-foot house in the middle of my 200-acre horse ranch. I still have that school paper framed over the fireplace." THE END.

"He added, 'The best part of the story is that two summers ago that same schoolteacher brought thirty kids to camp out on my ranch for a week.' When the teacher was leaving, he said, 'Look, Monty, I can tell you this now. When I was your teacher, I was something of a dream stealer. During those years I stole a lot of kids' dreams. Fortunately, you had enough gumption not to give up on yours.'"[1]

THINKING IS THE HARDEST THING WE HAVE TO DO

Our imagination is the mental faculty that creates our future.

---

[1] Canfield, Jack. *Chicken Soup for the Soul 20th Anniversary Edition*, 2013.

Don't let anyone steal yours. It is the key to creating your life.

You see, I didn't know what I didn't know until I finally realized that I can be whatever I want! I have the choice to decide and the power to be and do whatever it is I can imagine. I can bring all of that which I can think to life. We have a choice to do and be anything we want, but as we get older how do we imagine a life that's different from the one that we already have?

Thomas Edison put it clearly when he said, "One of the hardest things to do is imagine, and most humans do not do it." This is a critical part of what we want, so why don't we do it more often?

We are not taught how to use our imaginations as we grow, or how to use visualization as a tool for that matter. Learning to use your imagination despite not learning how to do it in school starts with asking yourself what you would love. If you could *do* or *be* anything, what would that look like? We'll talk more about this, and there is an exercise to help you get started at the end of this chapter. Note: One of my favorite essential oils to use while developing imagination is "Envision."

DESIRE FOR HAPPINESS

A young lady named Debra came to me, and she was on what I call the "wheel of life." You may be familiar with that wheel. Day in and day out, we do the same thing over and over again, hoping and praying that something will give or change. Yet it never does, and it won't. What you are waiting for is the circumstance to change so you can take action. Let me ask you, as I asked the young lady that came to me, how long have you been waiting for the circumstance to change? Ouch. Clients have said two to three years, and some have said seventeen to twenty, but the scariest is when they say their whole lives—of which they are now in their sixties and seventies.

I often ask, "Do you have life or does life have you? If you are on this wheel and you long for happiness, and you know happiness is out there, yet you keep waiting for something to happen so life changes, believe me: it won't. What has to change is you." We fear change more than we desire to be happy. I don't know what is scarier: waiting for years for something to change—and never seeing what you need to do in order to change—or taking that a step and risking what "could" happen as you dare to achieve your dreams. That dream is happiness and peace. We all deserve it.

Debra is thirty-two and knows that this wheel of life may kill her and could destroy her marriage—to the person who once was the love of her life and has now become her partner in a never-ending fight. They fight about money, work hours, kids, and so on and so on. She and her husband have both turned into nagging, undesirable people. Along with this conflict, of course, there is this deep understanding of not wanting to give up. Instead of blaming and defending, how about admitting responsibility and looking inside—not at what the others can do to change but how *you* have to change.

There are choices, yes; this is a choice. I am certain what's happening for Debra just isn't happening in her marriage but is also happening in relationships with family, friends, and coworkers. Remember that *how you do one thing is how you do everything*. The battle is not with your spouse; it's with yourself. You can go from relationship to relationship, and still the same situation will arise. The outward happiness you are seeking through that person is only temporary. Seeking happiness, joy, and love comes with a realization that it is "I" that needs to change, and I change the circumstance to create what I want. Getting off the wheel of life means stepping out and taking a chance on something new that can potentially change the circumstances that surround you, taking a risk in the direction of your dream to *do more* and *be more*.

You can relate to this, right? We all want to be happy, yet so many are not, and it is so sad. Debra took the risk and began to think about what she wanted in life—not just broad and big, more like a blueprint—and she began to create the design. What could I do to help? I worked with Debra to create her design, and she realized in the process that maybe she didn't always say what she wanted. She was timid and shy, never wanting confrontation. Over time, she assumed others understood when really they didn't. Time after time Debra was disappointed, and with that comes resentment. How was it that Debra created her results?

No one likes confrontation, but it exists. You can choose to rise above it and get results, or you can let it hold you back for years. In the event of confrontations or heated arguments, you first must imagine, think about, and see the results you want, NOT just react or allow your mouth to run without realizing what you are saying. You can choose to rise above, but it's you who has to change.

When we simply allow things to happen to us—without creating and imagining—there is an incongruence in who we truly are. How could anyone have peace, happiness, and joy when they are out of sync with who they really are? You can fake it, sure. Let me know how that works for you. If you want to change your life and begin living with the limitless possibilities of your imagination, it's not everyone else around you that must change—it's you!

HORSES AND INCONGRUENCE

If we took Debra into the arena with horses, it would look like incongruence. You might be wondering how this shows up. Well, if we are unsure of what we want, we can walk around aimlessly and feel like we are getting results when, in the end, we aren't getting anything at all. What if we set up an obstacle course in the arena, however—with maybe a barrel to go around, a pole to walk over, and some cones to weave through? Stay with me, now. Debra may look at the obstacles and be unsure of what is next.

So the conversation sounds like this: "You said you just want happiness." So happiness is all of these things, right? Metaphorically the barrel is her family of love and joy, the pole to work over is her career (and what an amazing one it is), and the cones are all the jobs she has to do through the day. "Simple! Take the horse and go around the barrel, over the pole, and weave through the cones, and when you're done, you'll feel happiness."

Does it work? Of course not.

But why not? Well, it's because we haven't identified what happiness is. Society says we need a family, we need a good career, graduate school, to buy a house, and so on. They are not necessarily in that order, and all of those things are good things. However, you must decide what would make *you* happy.

IMAGINE

Let's bring that back in: What if the barrel represented harmony, respect, and cooperation within the family. The career is fulfilling, creative, and challenges you—which brings the money you've always wanted, the bills are paid, and there is freedom to work on your hobbies and be with your family. The cones represent all the things you do for yourself, like working with a life coach, exercising, going on girls retreats and getting a massage once a month.

With imagination comes vibration. The vibration and

visualization was clear. The vibration of happiness, increased desire, and longing pulled Debra forward, and she visualized having it all. That visualization felt good, therefore the course was a breeze. When she got focused on what she wanted and clearly defined it, that image gave her the motivation she needed to succeed. This strategy can work for you as well if you clearly define and visualize what you want and allow that longing to pull you forward, continually motivating you to succeed.

PLANNING

You heard me say earlier that when we do what we love, long for, and desire, the heart rate increases, we feel good, and we may even lose track of time. When we're happy and surrounded by positivity, we're more likely to attract even more positivity and create more happiness. Do you see now how important this is?

Let start by creating a vision. Do you remember a time when you were planning a vacation? For some, this could take hours, days, months, and even years. I know people who plan vacations several years in advance. Regardless of how much time you take in planning this vacation, you searched the web, stopped at the travel agent, talked to friends and neighbors, and did a whole lot of in-depth research before you decided where you would go.

The next step to consider is how to get where you're going. For some, a train would be a great adventure—and maybe the trip you just imagined even changed because you'd never thought of taking a train before. If you *could* get there by train, think of what you could see on the way! Think about going across the country and ending in Alaska. This is tough stuff planning, but what an incredible adventure with views and activities along the way!

Okay, you've figured out where and how, but now you need to think about what you will do there. Read a book? Well, if you are going to Alaska, one thing you could do is to explore the history of the gold rush, or maybe the history of the natives there and what their life is like. Maybe you could explore the local animals and go on a fishing expedition. I would I love to see the whales and sea animals that live there. It would be amazing to watch them for endless hours, just experiencing their beauty. That's what I would do on my vacation because that's what would make me feel good. What would you do on yours?

We're not done yet! Where will you stay? You've decided where you'll go, how you'll get there, and what you will do once you arrive. Are you going to sleep in a tent, a hotel, or maybe event rent an RV and travel about? And don't forget that there are certain things that will need to be taken care of before you leave. Maybe you'll need to pay the bills a week earlier, get your dog to your sister's place while you are away, set the timers on the lights in the house so it looks like someone is home, and make sure all your work on your desk is done—even if this means staying late at work and working weekends for about six weeks. There's even more than all of that to think about. What about the meeting that is happening the day you return to work? You'll need to prepare for that ahead of time and have everything ready before you go. There's so much to think about and decide! I bet you didn't even think twice about just how much effort all of this entails—you just do it. Why? Because it's fun, brings you happiness, and saturates you with a feeling of fulfillment. It increases your heart rate and makes you feel content—you're doing something you love.

Okay, now that we've talked about vacations, let's take this approach to other areas of your life, such as your health, career, relationships, and time/money freedom. Relationships are a part of everything we do, so let's start there. If you closed your eyes and thought about relationships, what would your ideal one look like? What would the marriage you long to have look like? What about the relationships with your children, your parents, your sister, and your boss?

Identify the relationship you want with your spouse. Think about things you desire, such as clear communication, someone who is supportive of your ideas, someone who won't judge you but rather encourages you, someone who is a good listener, and someone who understands your needs. Do you see my point? You can apply these criteria to every relationship.

Let's take this discussion back to the arena. How do a herd of horses demonstrate relationship ties? Well, I see them staying close together, swatting flies off of each other, grooming each other, and watching over each other for danger. Now take that information and apply it to a human and horse relationship. If I showed up, threw a halter on the horse, hassled it into the arena, and ordered it to get busy, what would that look like? Yucky! That's not the kind of relationship that you described wanting with others at all. Here we go back to the congruence. Does the external me show up, or does the inner me take control? Does pride or ego play a part in my decisions?

Having a "me" agenda and the "get 'er done" attitude has no place in relationships. This is just the kind of attitude, in fact, that took me down at age thirty-five. I controlled, pushed, and made things happen without realizing the impact these actions were having on me. I didn't understand what it was doing to me mentally, emotionally, and spiritually—and by thirty-five, I was in the hospital having a heart catheterization.

I'm a lot more relaxed now, and this is true of my relationships with horses as well as people. If I take time to ask permission to enter the stall (bedroom, house, work office, etc.) and he acknowledges me, then I can go enter the horse's space. I can ask him to place his nose in the halter and join me for a session. I may groom him a little, walk him, and stretch him some—maybe give him a treat to encourage a positive session—and then we are off. How do you think that session will go?

Well, I can tell you! It will go so much better than the one where I just abruptly rushed the horse to the arena. Why? Because I put the importance of our relationship first. He will be more willing to do things for me, will offer me more, and will want to be with me more than if I had just gone in there and "gotten it done."

I remember a time when my husband would just storm into the kids' rooms to get them moving on their chores. What he was thinking, I have no idea. When he was willing to hear the children explain why they didn't want to do their chores, it turned out that it was because he *demanded*. Think about it. If I demand something, it causes an immediate wall to form, and the defenses come up. Imagine that same scenario with a slight change now. He knocks on the door and then enters, asking if they could get on their chores. No yelling, no demanding. What would the reaction be now? I imagine the request would be much better received. Do you get what I'm saying?

CREATING YOUR CAREER

Let's apply this same principle in envisioning your career. What does this career look like? Is it an actual career, or a job? Do you love what you do, or do you dread Monday morning and can't wait until Friday comes? How you do one thing is how you do everything. Imagine if you could do anything and nothing—time, money, education, gender, age, marital status, etc.—was in the way. What would you love to do?

You might think:

I'd love a career that allows me to help people. I'd love to lift them up and inspire them to be the best they can be. I'd want to teach them how to break through all of the things that hold them back from achieving their goals. I'd love a career helping those people, and I know that time would just slip by because the passion in me ignites. This great job would bring me heartwarming love so abundant that I would have a wealth of happiness and positivity. Where would I find a career like this?

DISCOVERING WHAT'S WITHIN

This is where we go inside. All of the answers are within us. The greatest question I learned to ask was, "What can I do to move in the direction of my dream?" Maybe there's someone you can talk to. Take some educational or training courses and volunteer in an area that would connect you to what you'd love. Sharing your dream could also open possibilities you didn't know were there. There really is so much we can do—we just have to learn how to think about it. We can't think with what we know. We have to ask important, powerful questions for the mind to respond.

Remember that when the mind answers, you must respond. It's an opportunity. You have three seconds to do something— make a decision. Bam! When we live from within, amazing things happen without explanation. It just works. It's called "alignment within."

Essential Oils recommended:

Magnify Your Purpose™ essential oil blend stimulates creativity, desire, focus, and motivation, encouraging you to seize initiative when used aromatically.

Clarity™ blends basil, rosemary, peppermint, and other essential oils for an aroma that invites a sense of clarity and alertness.

Inspiration™ is a blend of pure essential oils that were traditionally used by native people of Arabia, India, and North America for enhancing spirituality and meditation.

Imagination Activity:

If I could wave a magic wand, what would I create or change?

_____

_____

What would love more of? If you're not sure, look at the next question first.

_____

_____

What would you like less of?

_____

_____

What gives your life meaning, where time passes and you are unaware?

_____

_____

What are you good at?

_____

_____

Don't think about what other people might think, and don't go into self-doubt or self-arguing over this. Write down the very first thing that comes to mind. This is allowing our intuition to guide us, not our over-thinking!

Chapter 3

Value of Specificity

If you think you can or you think you can't, you're right.

—Henry Ford

This is something we've sort of skirted around in previous chapters, but it's important enough to warrant its own discussion. I want to talk about the value of specificity: what it is, how it can help you, and where to begin.

WHAT IS SPECIFICITY?

I sure wish someone would have told me long ago how important it is to be specific in identifying what you want. Specificity is obviously the quality of being "specific." It's the process of taking a vague idea or abstract concept and breaking it down into concrete "ingredients." Let's think about this for a moment. Pretend that your goal in life right now is to "be happy." I can relate, and I'm sure almost everyone else reading this can, too. What does "being happy" mean to you? Does it mean having lots of alone time, or maybe spending a lot of time with friends at social events? What *specifically* has to happen in order to ensure that happiness?

It's not enough to talk about what kind of results you want to achieve, in other words. If you truly want those results, you have to identify them in detail. One example of how this works is the vacation we planned in the last chapter. We took the general idea of "going on vacation" and quickly broke it down into very specific destinations and activities. When we're working towards a relationship or career goal, however, this could be more challenging. Let's talk about those examples next.

SPECIFICITY IN CAREERS AND RELATIONSHIPS

Let's look at a career or a job. Do you want to go to that nine-to-five job where you sit at a pizza shop, wait on customers, and make nine dollars an hour? If so, that's great! But I'm willing to bet that the vast majority of you have simply defaulted to working because you have bills to pay, not because you're passionate about the work. In order to find happiness in your career, you have to start doing what you love. I'm going to be honest: this isn't easy in the beginning. It takes a lot of time to think about what you'd love to do every day. Once you can determine that, however, you can start to move forward with your life. What can you do with what you have to get the results for which you're looking?

For me, the most amazing career when it comes to helping people would be a counselor. Let's break the path to that career down and look at how you can go from the broad to the specific. First of all, what kind of counselor would you want to be? Think about the kinds of people you'd like to help—their ages, maybe, or their experiences. Now think about the kind of degrees and qualifications you need in order to get there. How many people do you think you can reach this way? Do you want to work for a practice or start your own? This is designing and planning. By going specific, you're creating the life that you'll love.

You can apply this same strategy to your relationships. This might be a harder subject to consider, but it's an important one. Let's think about your significant other. Are you with them because you genuinely love and respect them, or are you with them because you don't want to be alone? Or maybe you're with them because you think "it's time" for you to settle down, and they're available? Apply that line of questioning to your friends. How many people do you genuinely want to see and spend time with, and how many do you spend time with because it's the socially acceptable or easy thing to do?

It's time to get specific. What about that dream career? What, exactly, would it entail? What steps can you start taking in order to get to that point? Ask the same questions about your relationships. You might find yourself struggling to answer these questions—I get it. It's not easy, and it's especially difficult because it's not how society programs us to be. We're not really supposed to ask what will make us happy, but rather what we are able to accomplish and be successful doing. We're taught to value the external over the internal, in other words, and that need for external validation leads to stress, anxiety, and depression.

Don't stay stuck in that sinkhole! Start to think for yourself.

YOUR JOURNEY

It is said that one of the hardest things humans have to do is think—and that most don't do it. That doesn't mean that people don't think *about* things, but rather that the ability to be mindful about what you're thinking—to think about something with focus and deliberation—is incredibly difficult. This is a sentiment likely to be echoed by anyone who attempts meditation or yoga. One of the hardest things to do is to let go of your thoughts and simply live in the moment. That's because it's incredibly difficult to control your thoughts and focus upon one thing at a time—and yet, if we don't, we run the risk of falling into a routine of anxiety and fear.

If you should find yourself in that routine, the interesting thing is that you tend to stay there. You get caught up on your "wheel of life" where you do the same things every day. You see, the wheel of life is both external, as we discussed in the previous chapter, and internal. You allow your mind to run wild, indulge your worries and fears, engage in self-argument, and find yourself suffering from increasing amounts of stress and anxiety until you get to a place where you don't know *what* to do … just that we have to do *something*.

You need to break out of this pattern. In order to do that, you need to stop letting your mind run wild! You need to be mindful about your thoughts. To start getting specific, you have to start to "train" your mind to behave. Do you let your kids run all over the place, come home whenever they want, and hang out on corners? I don't think so. You have more control over your mind than you do your children, so why let it behave badly?

YOUR MIND – THE JUMPING MONKEY

In certain Eastern cultures, it is said that the mind is like a jumping monkey. One must tether it to tap into its power. Would you not like to tether your monkey? Of course you would! Feed it

51

the right food and water, and give it the knowledge it needs in order to keep growing. Make sure it gets a good amount of activity. If you don't exercise your mind, what happens? Well, your thinking becomes very limited. Much like your range of motion might be compromised if you don't exercise or move around often, your mind will begin to lose its "flexibility." Don't panic! Even if you're worried that your mind might be out of shape at the moment, there's still plenty of time to help it grow healthy and strong. Remember that all the answers for whatever we need are within ourselves—we just have to tap into them.

You might be thinking that you can't do this. Maybe you think it's just too difficult, or too foreign a concept. WRONG! The power is within every one of us. What you have to do now—what I want you focus on—is thinking mindfully and positively. Instead of thinking about what you hate, start thinking about what would make you happy. Give your mind the training it needs to thrive, and you'll soon reap the benefits.

I've said this before, and I'll say it again: people want peace, happiness, and joy. These are not objects—they are emotions. What makes you feel them? Really take the time to *think* about it. Do you remember the activity that you did in the first chapter? We talked about what you would love to do as a career. Pull that activity out and give it a look. Can you envision that job in your mind? That is the end result.

The most important thing we can do to harness the power of our minds is to think about our goals mindfully and develop specific milestones. We cannot get to where we want to go without first having a destination in mind. Mary Morrissey, my mentor and teacher, would often say that "a sailor doesn't set sail without a destination in mind." Neither should you! Stop trying to fix life, and start getting specific about what you want for your future. Don't worry about what the people around you might think. Who cares? This is *your* life! When you can put the need for external validation aside and focus on what you would truly love, life comes ALIVE!

Isn't that the kind of life you want to live? I don't know anyone who doesn't want feelings of peace, love, happiness, and joy. In order to have them, you need to get specific in the areas that would bring you those emotions.

SPECIFICITY WITH HORSES

How does this show up in horses? Think about a herd of horses out in the wild. These are prey animals, so they're always living in the present moment. They don't think about yesterday or worry about tomorrow because doing so could cost them their lives. Instead, they focus on the present. When they need food, they find a safe place and eat. When they need water, they seek some out. They know their paths, and they don't just wander around aimlessly. This is their life! If a mare is giving birth, they plan a place to have it, others support the mare in her labor, protect the area, and allow the mother to labor safely.

HORSE AND HUMAN

Kathy, a dear woman, came to me with worry, anxiety, and fear. Her thoughts were always stuck on the "what ifs," not on the specifics. She was putting herself in a rabbit hole every day! Thinking is your job—nobody else can do it for you. You choose what you want to think, yet every day she was deciding to think about things that caused her worry and stress. When we're constantly under that onslaught of negativity, the body is drained mentally and spiritually. Eventually, our health begins to be affected by it. Every single day she awoke, she was already worried.

I asked her to create a horseshoe in the arena. She could use anything in there to make it. The horseshoe was to represent the day, and the obstacles symbolized things about which she was worried. So in this case, the question was, "What do the obstacles represent for you?" She knew, but she didn't really understand how often worry took hold of her mind. Now that she sees the worry in physical form, however, she starts to have a conversation with herself. *Why would I do that? Why didn't I realize that?*

This is that "aha" moment. Now let's take the horse throughout your day. The horse represents you. If the obstacle course is too tight, what does that mean for you as you try to navigate the day? In this particular case, she realized it was impossible for her to complete the obstacle course because there were simply too many things in her mind that prevented her from getting what she wanted done. That realization is priceless. Her mind was busier they her doing.

What could she do differently? She has to think ... where? Inside. Yes, internally. She told me that if she stopped worrying so much, she could get more things done. So she went and removed the cones that represented worry. There were *nine* of them! Big difference, yes? Now could she do the course? Yes. However, if you can envision this course, she removed the cones of negative thinking so there were then huge gaps. She now could get through the beginning of the day and could do what she wanted or needed to do through creating more results.

You see, we can't see what we can't see until we are aware. During this activity, even though she knew she worried too much, she didn't realize *how much* worry she had and how it was controlling her life. Great stuff! Most importantly, when we take away an old pattern we have to put something there to create a new one. In this situation, Kathy began with exercising and going for a walk each morning, something she never had time to do before when paralyzed by worry.

Was she okay with this for the time being? Could she do it differently? There are so many ways to consider, but it's not for us to judge. In thinking about your life and goals, where can you get more specific about what you want out of life instead of just wandering around? When you take the time to identify those things that are holding you back by occupying all the space in your mind, you can finally remove them, just like Kathy did with the nine cones. Then you are able to replace those negative, self-limiting thoughts of worry and anxiety with positive ideas, creative energy, and limitless imagination. You can tether the jumping monkey of your mind and harness its power to find the answers within and do great things!

Essential Oils I recommend:

Frankincense essential oil has an earthy, uplifting aroma that's perfect for grounding and spiritual connectedness. Create a safe and comforting environment when you diffuse or inhale this empowering oil—a perfect opportunity to collect your thoughts. When you seek purpose or engage in prayer or meditation, use this oil to enhance your experience.

Rosemary is a familiar herb with a strong woodsy scent that can promote feelings of clarity.

The blend of essential oils found in **Hope™** brings an aroma that invites you to restore your faith by reconnecting with feelings of strength and stability.

Creating Specificity Activity:

Imagine a slowly moving picture. You've waved the magic wand over your dream, but now see it in slow motion. What are the details? Don't worry about the now versus the impossible. Just stay with me and imagine.

Trust the process.

That relationship/career you want, what would you love?

_____

_____

_____

Is there someone you can talk to who would help you?

_____

_____

_____

What would be required of you to reach your dream? Is it more school, a study program, certification, or practice?

_____

_____

_____

What are three action steps you could take in order to move in the direction of your dream?

_____

_____

_____

As you do this, the mind will think more thoughts of what you would truly love. If you are thinking something different about creating your life, then make notes.

What would you really want? List as many as possible and weed out until you have what you'd love.

_____

_____

_____

_____

_____

_____

_____

_____

_____

_____

_____

_____

_____

_____

_____

_____

_____

_____

_____

_____

_____

_____

_____

_____

Chapter 4

Your Decisions Have Weight

We can't solve our problems with the same thinking we used when we created them.
—Thomas Edison

How we do one thing is how we do everything. Many spend too much of their time in the phase of worry, fear, and doubt. I was there!

What you need to understand is that indulging in this worry isn't going to help anything. Allowing your subconscious to run amok is only going to get you in the habit of not making mindful decisions. Think about your mind and how your thoughts tend to develop. How do you think problems arise? It all starts with not being able to walk the walk when creating the life you want.

Don't ask why you can't have happiness and success. Figure out what those things mean to you, and decide to consciously work towards them as goals every day.

What you think is what you create. You can have it all—you just have to decide to go for it.

CREATE YOUR HAPPINESS

Let's place all of your worry, stress, fear, doubt, and self-arguing on a shelf for a moment. Why spend time worrying about this stuff? You should know there's nothing out of your reach. You can do this. So let's shelve the negative emotions for a bit.

Go get several pieces of paper. On them, write down all the things of which you want to rid yourself. The mind MUST SEE IT. Leave big spaces in between each word because you're going to cut them apart. You can also use one of those block square note pads. Write one thing on each piece of paper, and make sure you grab enough paper to see the project through! I'm pretty sure I used a ream the first time I did this.

Take your time and really think! You might be surprised at what comes out. One thing that resonated within me, for example, was the desire to stop feeling the need to prove myself to everyone. That's something that has really helped me, and it's something that I never would have realized I needed to do if I hadn't taken the time to delve into my own mind. As you mindfully evaluate the things you can remove from your life, you will make room for what would bring you happiness.

BUILD STRONGER RELATIONSHIPS

The above activity has helped me create stronger ties with my loved ones—especially with my husband. We were going through a "grow" period, and I was focused on ME. During that time, it seemed that everything he did was wrong.

You know what I'm talking about. Ladies, we are just always

right—right? Well, I had to let that belief go. One year during the winter, I wrote down all of the things that were irritating me about my husband. I included things like his lack of communication, ignorance, poor attitude, lack of cooperation, lack of interest, lack of support, and on and on and *on*. On the flip side of this activity, I wrote down all of his great qualities. Oh my heavens! You can't imagine this. The mind cannot possibly see it without writing it down. There where so many characteristics that I had to stop writing them down. I had been so focused on his negative behavior that I blew them up into something that completely obscured all of the good thoughts I had about him. Does this sound familiar?

Let's get back to that shelf now. We are going to permanently shelve some stuff about you. Write down everything, and be honest. Why would you even consider lying to yourself?

Yeah, well, we all do it. We lie to ourselves more than we do other people, even. So go deep, and write down everything. The more you put into this, the more you get out. You might want to do this exercise over a period of a couple days because as you begin to write things down, more things will come to mind. It's almost as though the floodgates have opened—you'll have a steady stream of things to write down once you get started.

Once you have written everything down, put that paper into a box. If you're really seriously about this, then take that box outside. Realize that it symbolizes everything that you want to rid yourself of, and it's time to let the universe know you mean business. Now take a lighter and burn the box. This is a huge undertaking, and I know it can be scary. These are pieces of your life that you want to burn away! Make that honest decision to harness your life and create the kind of life you want to lead.

CONTROL YOUR LIFE

Excellent. Great job! I am truly proud of you, and I know that wasn't easy. But now you can move on. You might even feel lifted and free! You've created an open space—like an empty room—in your mind, within which you can begin creating something new.

At this point, you've decided to take control of your life. Now you have to think about what will take place every day. It's time to get creative and plan your future! Your control depends on conscious awareness, what it is that you are thinking. We've already talked about how you have the power to create your ideal life—it all depends upon your thinking. A great book to go even deeper with this idea is *Power of Decision* by Raymond Charles Barker. He says it takes courage to shake off the routines of comfort and start adventuring with the control of your life.[2] He's right!

When we decide to take control, a new adventure will begin. Can you see it? There are unlimited possibilities. Once you start practicing mindfulness, you'll begin to realize that the thoughts you need to have always seem to pop up right when you need them. Your mind will help you create the life you want.

BE AWARE

We are all able to think, choose, and decide. If you think, "I never get a break," then you won't take any breaks. If you think, "This only happens to me," then it will seem as though it only happens to you. On the flip side, if you think, "Life is going to give me good things," then it will! Does this mean we won't hit bumps in the road? Of course not. We'll all experience difficulties—that's

---

[2] Barker, Raymond Charles. *Power of Decision: A Step-By-Step Program to Overcome Indecision and Live Without Failure Forever*. New York: Penguin, 1968.

part of life. But the important takeaway here is that your life can be significantly *less* difficult if you start to make mindful decisions to be happy and stress-free. We are the ones who decide life is hard. We make the process of change difficult on ourselves. Interesting, right? I never used to look at it that way, but once I started to, everything changed.

Make decisions to give up the excuses, develop a new perception, and be careful. Only you choose to have a failure-prone life. You let things happen. You may not think so, but you do. You need to accept responsibility for your life, quit blaming the world, and start taking action to harnessing the life you want to live. Focus on what you want, the person you want to *be*, and the things you want to *do* that will make you happy.

MINDFULNESS AND HORSES

How does the concept of mindfulness show up for horses? Remember that they're prey animals. Their entire life depends on survival, and in a split second they can live or die. The same can happen for humans as well—we know this. What's the difference between humans and horses?

Do you think that horses have the time to talk their decisions over with a friend? Do they think about how many beasts are out there that can attack them? Do they wonder if they will be attacked every time they move? NO! They immediately look at a situation or thought and make a decision within seconds. If a stallion is looking for attention and the mare says no, what does that look like? Bam! Kick, done. It is decided, clear, and focused with action that gets the needed results.

How does this show up with a horse and human? It's really quite amazing how horses know all this stuff intuitively versus how complicated humans make it. Take a situation that leaves you unsure about the right decision. I've laid out a course where the participants need to simply step over a four-foot pole, walk clockwise around the barrel, and weave through four tall six-foot poles.

Simple, yes? Did I mention that you and the horse have to do this course together? All you need to do is decide what you're going to do. It's simple. Decide what to do and the horse will walk with you. If you're reluctant, unsure, or have any doubt, do you think the horse will go with you? Think of the horse as being your subconscious. Externally you say, "I'm in," but internally you say, "Well, maybe once I finish the first project up, I'll do this." When your inside doesn't match your outside, the horse (your subconscious) is confused and has no idea what you want. This is why making a firm, focused decision is so important.

When you commit 100 percent, your horse will willingly walk with you. Your thoughts and your desires will be in harmony with each other, and everything will fall into place.

Essential Oils I recommend:

Valor for every morning to greet the day with a positive attitude or to unwind at the end of the day. Its powerful yet calming scent is versatile enough that you can integrate it into your morning and bedtime routines and anywhere in between.

Believe™ contains Idaho Blue Spruce, Idaho Balsam Fir, Frankincense, and other essential oils that may encourage feelings of strength and faith when used aromatically.

The sweet fragrance of **Inner Child™** can be used aromatically to encourage you to connect with your authentic self.

Decisions Have Weight Activity:

What do you do in a day that is in the direction of your dream?

_____

_____

_____

What goals do you need to decide on to bring the results you want?

_____

_____

_____

What areas of your life would you like to improve or change?

_____

_____

_____

What do you need to do to be 100 percent committed to growing and changing?

_____

_____

_____

What do you need to do for yourself in order to move forward with your dream?

_____

_____

_____

Chapter 5

Obstacles You Will Face

The mind is everything. What you think, you become.

—*Buddha*

On your journey there will be times when obstacles overwhelm you. Sometimes it might even feel like someone is throwing them in your way. When the going gets good, the obstacles tend to show up in spades to complicate life—and they show up from the strangest of places.

COMPLICATIONS AND DELAYS

When I worked in the real estate industry, I ran into the issue of unexpected complications all the time. Whenever I thought I had the best client—a win/win deal and a piece of cake—the obstacles would come crawling out of the woodwork. Here's an example: I have a prequalified couple and their credit is perfect. They have a

10 percent deposit and are buying a lovely 2,000-square-foot home for $325,000. They love the cultured stone in the front, the two-car garage to store their toys and vehicles, and the pool in the backyard that the kids will just love. They also have several quads that the family goes trail riding with, a motorhome, and a trailer for the quads, as well as the GMC that tows the trailer. It seems like a match made in heaven, in other words, and the family is excited. The parents both have good jobs. Their application is filed, the deposit is in, the contract is out of review, and home inspection is underway—everything is moving along nicely. With that said, however, one problem presents itself: Even though they have great credit, they are borderline up to the max as far as their income-to-debt ratio goes. They cannot acquire any more debt, or it could put them over the edge.

Then the home inspection report comes back, and there is radon in the home. The family is devastated. They go into crisis mode and can't believe this is happening to them. Everything always happens to them, I've heard them lamenting, and things never go right. They have already packed half of their other home, started filling out the forms to change their address, and then the report comes in and everything stops. Their first response is that they can't buy the house. They want to kill the deal. Let me point out a few things we talked about in earlier chapters regarding the importance of having a vision, being specific in what you want, and the importance of making a decision. What just happened to the family? They lost their vision, forgot about the specifics, and changed their decision. There was no forward momentum but rather high-speed reverse.

THE IMPORTANCE OF MAINTAINING MOMENTUM

Never give up on what you want. Thomas Edison conducted thousands of experiments before he invented the light bulb. Thousands! Can you imagine? Most people will give up after one to three attempts at something new—if it doesn't work out right away, the majority of individuals will drop it and move on to something else. We get more focused on the problems—the ways in which something *isn't* working out—than we do on how it *is* working. Instead, we must learn to focus on solutions rather than problems, and maintain our forward momentum.

Think about it: creating success is all about maintaining a continual upward spiral. A forward spiral, not backwards, right? If we always look at solutions rather than obstacles when it comes to a specific situation, which direction are we going in? That's right, we're moving forward. We're maintaining that forward momentum. Whether you believe it or not, there is always a solution to everything. Now there may come a time when we don't particularly *like* the solution, but there is always at least one solution. Always look forward.

Moving back to the family interested in buying a house, we've had a specialist come in and tell the soon-to-be new homeowners that there is an old well in the basement that is open and allowing radon to come into the house. The recommendation was that the well in the basement was not necessary and could be closed up. That's it—just like that, the problem is solved.

How much stress did the family members cause their collective mind, heart, blood pressure, and body when their first response was crisis mode? What were they looking at? The answer is simple: they were focused on the problem. The problem was radon in the house, and the family couldn't see beyond this issue. When they looked for a solution rather than a problem, however, they found that the answer was very simple and cost less than two hundred fifty dollars.

Yes, there was an obstacle, but it was very simple to overcome. You'd be surprised how often this is the case, if we can just look forward instead of freezing at the unexpected. When we consider the idea of being open to a good outcome, even if it's not the exact outcome we anticipated, we avoid a lot of unnecessary stress.

DON'T BE YOUR OWN OBSTACLE

Let me give you another example. One of the biggest obstacles we all face in life—and this is a huge one—is ourselves. We are our biggest critics. We love to worry, talk ourselves out of things because we can't see the whole picture, even ask all our friends for their opinion, and then never take a step in the direction of what we want.

If you could focus not only on solutions but also be open to any positive outcome, how do you think your life would change? Let go of any negative thought patterns you may have, the self-criticism, and just step forward. Take one step every day in the direction of your dream and amazing things will begin to happen.

I love what philosopher Henry David Thoreau says about this: "If one advances confidently in the direction of their dreams, and endeavors to live the life which he has imagined, he will meet with success unexpected in common hours." All of the self-talk and negative thinking that we tend to indulge in just holds us back like vise grips, and then people wonder why they feel stuck. We can be our own biggest obstacles, but I know that you can overcome any obstacles when you decide to look forward and be open to any positive outcome.

When you are open to different outcomes and keep your eyes on your vision, you can overcome any obstacle that comes your way. The passion for what you want will drive you forward. Like a car, sometimes you will weave a little to the right or to the left, but you just have to remember to get right back on the road again. Sometimes you might encounter traffic, sometimes fog, and sometimes you'll even find yourself stuck in the middle of a rainstorm. What do you do when you're driving and encounter these issues? You keep going. You move more cautiously, of course, but very few people stop driving altogether when things like this occur. You have things to do, after all. Can you really afford to just stop driving?

Of course not! You know you need to get things done. The drive to do what needs to be done and continue with your plans pulls you forward and keeps you moving.

FORWARD MOMENTUM AND HORSES

How does this show up in horses? The horse's language is very much a universal one. You can see it in everything they do if you just pay attention.

Here's a scenario. The horse and you are walking along the road and run into a creek. Now the creek could be really big and deep, or it could be very small and shallow. It doesn't really matter. The day is beautiful, the wind is blowing softly, the sun is shining, and crossing the creek would be refreshing. When you come to the creek, however, the horse halts. The horse has no depth perception, so you can see why it stops. The more interesting question is what you do once the horse stops. Do you give up and go another way, or do you push forward towards that refreshing feeling that the creek would afford? Are you thinking of driving off the road, in other words, or maintaining your forward momentum?

It's scary to cross the creek, especially when you're not sure what will happen. There could be some resistance. Maybe the other side is not what you wanted anyway. That's a possibility, of course. But more importantly, *what if it were?* What if the other side of the creek were exactly what you were hoping for?

With confidence, I decide to stick to my vision, make a decision, and keep moving into the water. I can feel the horse's body tense up, and I let him know that some steps ahead will be scary, but it will be okay because the rewards are huge. We just need to keep looking forward. Another step is taken, and he lets out a soft sigh. Before you know it, that intense feeling goes away, and we casually walk through the sunshine across the creek. The green pastures on the other side are full of nutrients. I felt lifted, inspired, and empowered to keep moving forward.

There will always be obstacles in the way, and they'll show up when you least expect them. What can you do to stay on the road of success? Keep your vision always in the forefront of your mind.

Write it down on three-by-five cards and keep a copy at your desk, one in your pocket or purse, one on the bathroom mirror, and one on your dash in the car. This will help you stay on your road to success. Do what you can with what you have, and just take a step forward every day.

Obstacles Activity:

What obstacles are you currently facing?

_____

_____

_____

What steps can you take forward?

_____

_____

_____

Is there someone you can talk to that would help you?

_____

_____

_____

Is there a skill you need to learn in order to move forward?

_____

_____

_____

How will you know you have overcome this obstacle?

_____

_____

_____

Chapter 6

Trusting the Process and Leaving Worry Behind

Your control depends upon your conscious awareness that your individual subconscious mind is a law of cause and effect. Nothing has ever happened to you or taken place around you that was not the result of your mind.

—Raymond Charles Barker, author of *The Power of Decision*

Trusting the process and leaving worry behind is a challenge for many people. In fact, it might seem nearly impossible! Remember that the mind is so powerful that it has over 15,000 thoughts a day. Of those thoughts, how many of them are self-talk, self-doubt, and worry—*What should I do? What do others think? What if my family doesn't like my decision?* This is the kind of self-talk that drains our energy and limits us unnecessarily. I wish more people realized the enormous amount of strain that worry and anxiety can have upon the body as well as the mind.

Let's look at ourselves for a moment. We are a luminous light, and we are energy. We have a field of influence and energy around us that most people don't understand and of which they aren't even aware! Where do we get energy from? You already know the answer. We all already know the answer! We must sleep seven to eight hours a night, put good food in our bodies, read inspiring and motivational books, exercise, and think positive thoughts—and the energy field is glowing like a circle of white light around you. Beautiful!

Here's an example. Your body is like a car, and when the car needs gas, you fill it up. You know this is a must because if you don't do this, the car will stop moving. With the gas, you can see, feel, and touch the moving car and the energy it exudes. Without the gas, nothing happens. It stands still and is lifeless. If you look at your body like a gas tank and you fill it with the proper fuel, you are filled with energy. You run well, you are happy, and life is good. The gas represents the healthy food, positive thoughts, exercise, etc.

What do you think happens when we worry? What about self-talk of "what if" and doubt? What do you think happens to the energy field? Well, I'll tell you: it decreases.

I bet you know many people who walk around complaining that they are tired and utterly without drive or inspiration. In fact, they probably spend a lot of time talking about what someone else did or didn't do, how horrible it was, and why can't good things ever go their way. In the meantime, their body feels tired, they don't sleep, maybe they have migraines going on, severe sinus issues, and they overall plain don't feel well. One of my mentors calls these people "negativists."

79

NEGATIVISTS

When we give the car gas, it runs. When we overuse something, what happens? It starts to break down. Will the car break down if you overuse and abuse it?

Let's add worry to the negativists, because the body will respond to it the same way as it does the complaining. It will drain our glowing light and energy, which will decrease so much that it's often hard to get it back again. Over time, it will become harder and harder to change our old ways. That's not to say it's impossible, of course, so don't worry if you find yourself in this position!

Overcoming worry and trusting in ourselves is the change and healing process. If you know that you told someone something and it was the honest truth, you believe it. You know it to be so and nothing anyone can say would change your mind because it's true. What if you applied that same principle to other areas of your life?

Let me help you. Your son or daughter goes off to college, and you know you've taught them, to the best of your ability, what they need to survive on their own. It is their job to take responsibility for their life, make good choices, and do the right things. Granted, there will come a time when maybe they will fall down. They sure as heck did when they were learning to walk. You recall watching them fall, crawl over into the coffee table and pick themselves back up again. They did it. What changed when they got to be ten or eleven? All of a sudden, you were doing the work for them. I know parents who will do their kids' homework if they didn't finish it. Really? What are they teaching their children? "No worries, when I can't do it, mom will." Really? No! This is where worry begins. We need to take responsibility for our own lives and let our children grow up.

Let's go back to our college example. The child leaves for college, and you do nothing but worry and worry. The kid is at college, having a blast. They are excited meeting new friends, experimenting with freedom, and—yippee!—living with no parents. They are having fun and mom is worrying. Does this sound good? No, and it's not. Trusting the process is knowing that when the child falls, they will crawl to the couch or table and get back up. That's what we taught them when they were small. They did it on their own.

You have to look forward. Worry makes you look backward and use up energy that is necessary for other parts of your life. You are worrying, in most cases, about something you have no control over. Do you see that? You have no control over the issue, but you still decide to worry about it anyway. This is a big thing for many people. You make the choice to worry. I don't know about you, but I sure as heck don't worry and would much rather choose to trust the process.

TRUSTING THE PROCESS AND HORSES

How does this show up in horses and humans? They are animals of prey, always on alert, and the impulse to fight-or-flight pops up whenever necessary.

Do they stand around worried, though? No. They are always present and in the moment. Taking time to worry could very well cause a delay in responding and open them up to being attacked. Worry could very literally kill them. There is so much to learn from the horse.

Let's take, for example, that your child is at college and you're worried all the time. They haven't returned your calls or contacted you, and you're all sorts of stressed out. This is the metaphor in the arena. There are no obstacles in front of you—just a horse with two lead lines. Your job is to move the horse from behind and walk forward around the arena. You're kind of like the cart with the reins: now focus forward and the horse will go.

What is the first thing that comes to mind? How? NO, not how! What can you do with what you have? What do you do? Remember that we talked about being a light force of energy. Can you use your energy here? Direct the horse to just start walking, because he will.

Worry honestly does us no good. Take that energy and convert it to positive meditation. Don't think you can't. Your meditating already just on worry instead of something positive. Whatever the thought is, flip it. Here, let me give you a few examples.

I know I'll just sleep the day away.	I am up and doing great things.
I probably won't get the job	I have all the experience necessary.
I don't like to drive on the highway.	I can drive on the highway and see amazing things.
I have no time to do what I want	I am doing what I want and have more time.

When you flip your thoughts from the negative (worry) to the positive (energy/light force), you will see a shift, both physically and mentally. You will reap the many benefits of a positive energy field that radiates peace and trust in every situation.

Essential Oils I recommend:

The powerful scent of **Motivation™** may promote feelings of action and accomplishment when diffused.

Forgiveness™ contains an aroma that supports the ability to forgive yourself and others while letting go of negative emotions, an important part of personal growth.

White Angelica™ contains pure Melissa and Bergamot essential oils, promotes feelings of protection and security when diffused, and can be used to guard against negative energy.

Trust and Leave Worry Activity

1. What do you find yourself worrying about? List as many items as possible.

_____

_____

_____

_____

_____

2. Now take time to flip all the worries and start the positive statements with "I am ___."

_____

_____

_____

_____

_____

3. Create an image here and be specific. If your life didn't have worry in it, what would that look like? How would it make you feel? What would you be doing? Where would you be?

_____

_____

_____

_____

_____

Chapter 7

Being Open to Outcome, Not How

Passion is powerful. It is a surge of energy that has nothing to do with commitment, determination, resolve, or a hardy hunger for getting what you don't have. Passion is what keeps you moving. It's the juice in the battery; it's what keeps you up at night, puts color into works and words in my head and heart. Passion is what will drive you.

—Michael Gerber, author of *E-Myth Mastery*

Life is so challenging sometimes.

We all go through life just trying to figure things out, and most of us don't have a clue as to what our life purpose is. We aren't taught to discover life's purpose. In fact, if I think back to my childhood and school days, I can't say this was a question that was ever asked of me, or even one that I ever considered.

Many of us are expected to follow in family traditions or, at the very least, do what our parents want us to do. Why do they care so much? Well, because they probably lacked a path themselves and assume that we must be similarly lost. Think about that. Through our thoughts and feelings, we make decisions based on what others want us to do rather than encouraging ourselves to follow our hearts and our passions. I know so many people who have amazing talent, and yet they aren't utilizing their gifts at all in their day-to-day lives. Think about a gifted pianist, for example, working as a banker because his family thought it was a better, more "stable" option than pursuing his passion and talent.

I can give you another good example. I have several friends and family members who are amazing artists. You can't image what they can do in thirty minutes, whether it's with a pen and paper or with a piece of wood and a knife. The most unbelievable pictures come from the work of their minds and hands, and yet they do nothing in this profession. Hmm, why do you think that is?

Part of the reasoning behind it is they don't know **how**. They will ask themselves over and over again: *but how would I do that?* How could I make a living doing that? How would I provide for my family? And interestingly enough, parents, teachers, and friends all let them know that field they want to enter doesn't make any money. They tell the aspiring dreamers that they need to do something else. They emphasize that the field offers no sustainable career opportunities and no benefits. They say it's better in the short term. You can do that as a hobby, not a career.

DREAM STEALERS

I call these people dream stealers. All of those people can predict the future, apparently, and somehow know everything there is to know about artists and their world. People love to give

87

opinions as though they are facts when, in reality, they honestly know nothing about the field in question (other than their readily given opinion, that is). They might know people who have given up on being an artist for various reasons, for example, and this will stay in their minds. To them, this is what an artist looks like: someone defeated and ready to give up on their dream. Remember that there is good and bad in everything. There is balance, yin and yang, dark and light. The important thing to do is to notice the good. The people offering their opinions, was it good or bad? Was it right or wrong?

What we think (vision) and what we focus upon dictate the results that we get. We have to learn to use our own minds, not the opinions of others. Granted, it's fine—perhaps a good idea, even, depending upon the field and the person in question—to hear what others have to say. In the end, however, use your own mind and follow your heart.

USE ALL YOUR SENSES

God gave us six mental faculties for a reason. They aren't just decoration; no, you're supposed to use them. Are you using them only when in survival mode, or are you using them as a barometer to life? Following your passion and your heart means listening to the small voice within us—the gut feelings—and heeding the so-called coincidences that show up. Your mental faculties include:

1. Thought
2. Will
3. Perception
4. Imagination
5. Intuition

6. Reason

Albert Einstein called this tapping into the intuitive mind, and it is the power behind our greatness and genius. And yet we so often do not use our minds in a way that will give us the answers we need.

THINK ABOUT ACTION

Let's look at this for a moment. Remember, there is power in you to do whatever you want as long as you can first think it. So we think it. I want to be a movie star. How could I?

Let's stop there; the correct train of thought should be more like: *What would I have to do to become a movie star?* You sit down and look at where you are versus where you want to be. As you learn, there are scary steps in the middle and challenges along the way. Your own thinking or reasoning will look at the barometer and see it as too uncomfortable to pursue. You'll want to just forget it and stay in your comfort zone. This is too big, forget it. NO. Everything in you screams to stay comfortable. What next?

Make a list of what it would take for you to become a movie star. No one can tell you that you can't do it. There are amazing stories out there about actors who were told they were never going to make. Take Jim Carrey, for example. Look at his story. He was what one could term "a nobody." Every day he envisioned himself as a movie star. In his dreams, he stood on the mountain top with a $1 million check written out to him time and time again, day in and day out. He believed in what he wanted even when all the cards were stacked again him. Where is he today? Jim Carrey is a successful actor, screenwriter, and producer, with roles in films such as *Dumb and Dumber*, *The Mask*, *Ace Ventura: When Nature Calls*, *Batman Forever*, *Liar Liar*, *How the Grinch Stole Christmas*, and *Bruce Almighty*. The list goes on and on, and it all came to life with a vision!

How about author Jack Canfield? After being turned down over 155 times, today—because of his belief in himself and his desire to follow his passion against all odds—he's a successful and internationally known author. A school teacher to an author, motivational speaker, seminar leader, corporate trainer, and entrepreneur. He is the co-author of the *Chicken Soup for the Soul* series, which has more than 250 titles and 500 million copies in print in over 40 languages, and the list goes on and on.

How about Babe Ruth? Did you know that in reaching the Hall of Fame, he had more strikeouts that year than home runs? There are so many people, so many examples. I can tell you the one thing they have in common is this: they never asked the question "HOW."

I know a young lady who is remarkably talented at the age of fourteen. Her mind and hands are more powerful than you can probably imagine. Some have tapped into their genius more easily than others. It's the same way that some glide through school while others have to study over and over and over to get good grades. Tapping in opens and unlocks that genius in us by asking questions like "What can I do with what I have in order to get the results I want?" Say that again. *What can I do with what I have in order to get ... a successful career in art, a book offer, more earning potential, an intimate loving relationship, a car, a new friend, a scholarship, (fill in the blank)?*

WHAT, NOT HOW

When we start to ask ourselves "what" and we quiet our minds, we start to think and are open to what happens next. Someone shows up, a call comes to you, an e-mail shows up in your inbox, oddly enough, at exactly the moment after you've posed a question to your genius. Hmm. Are you listening, or is your mind too busy thinking about all of the unnecessary worry, doubt, and planning instead of being present?

If you want to live the life you want, then you have to design it and see it come to life in order to find happiness, love, and joy. Then you have to stop, slow down, and learn new habits and patterns around what you want, not what you are. You're probably thinking that this is impossible. Well if it was, we wouldn't have so many successful people in life. There isn't anything you can't do. Plus, if you really think about it, success comes when you never give up and are willing to fall. Success requires you to have determination regarding what you want. Remember when you were a child and you wanted that bike? You didn't give up on it until you got it. You'd find all kinds of ways to ask your parents. You'd do anything to get it. Right? Darn straight.

We learn all of the traits we need, but then something happens and we fall off track. Then life starts evolving and, before you know it, we're on this wheel of life: unhappy, dissatisfied, unhealthy, and we don't know what to do.

Go back to chapters one and two. Creating results and having imagination is the beginning. Everything we do is created twice: first in thought, then in action. You cannot act without thought.

GET SPECIFIC

Writing a book, making a table, asking a girl on a date, going to the market, getting up, tying your shoe: everything starts with a thought. So start thinking about what you really want from life. What would you give anything to have in your life? What would you love to do? Then get specific. Get so specific that you could play it out in your head like a movie. Remember back in the day when movies first started, their creation involved one screen shot at a time showing a specific pose You could see every detail in the pictures. Yes! That's it. That's what you have to do. Get specific. If I wanted to be a movie star, for example, I'd ask:

1. What do I have to do to take action?
2. What talents do I have and how can I use them?
3. Where do actors live?
4. What film would I have had a supporting role in?
5. Who are my friends?
6. What new movie would I star in?

BE OPEN TO ANY OUTCOME

If you have passion and desire, you will believe in yourself and your dream and then start taking action. Do not try to figure out all of the pieces. That goes back to the "how" again. Be open to different outcomes. Plan for what you want, but be prepared when opportunity shows up whether you want it or not. You may run into someone who invited you to a book signing and you think, *I have no time*. WRONG! You make time. What if at that book signing for a friend, a producer is there and they introduce you? Oh my Gosh! Do you see what I mean?

Now you've met a producer, and you've gotten to know one another. Along the way the producer realizes you are a perfect fit for the movie another producer is doing and could help you land a star part. How would that make you feel? YES!

Being open to different outcomes means being aware of opportunity and how the universe tries to guide us and show us our path ... but we are the ones that continually get in the way. I mean that.

The only person holding you back is you. You can say whatever you think. If I had a conversation with you, you would have excuses and a perception that is not in alignment with your true reality. Your reasoning would talk you out of it, and you'd be asking questions like, "HOW?"

If you really want this, just start experimenting with it— especially since more opportunities will show up now that I've shared the importance of being more aware and always looking for opportunity. Remember: I said what you think about, focus on, and work to bring to action will give you results. It's the law of the universe, and it wants to work in harmony with you. You just have to allow it to do so.

Get out of your way. Stop the constant overthinking. Replace old habits with new ones. Learn something every day about what you can do to improve yourself. Improve who you are and others will follow. Do you know that person who is good at telling others what to do, and yet they don't do it themselves? Their life never changes. In order to change others, we have to change ourselves. No one will follow us where we haven't been. Hmm ... interesting.

Over the years, I have seen how using our minds and tapping into our genius is like unlocking a hidden door to life. It's fun, adventurous, uplifting, and truly amazing. My mind was hard and stubborn. I had to do things my way—the way I knew how—and I was always right. Do you know someone like that? For those people, I just get out of their way, and maybe you need to do the same for yourself. I was my biggest problem. I stood in my own way by not using my imagination, creating a vision of what I truly wanted, and being willing to go the extra mile. Here I am! If you would have asked me ten years ago what I would be doing today, my answer sure as heck wouldn't have included sitting here writing a book.

I may not have even been alive because my old ways of thinking and doing were causing major health concerns, and I not changed my ways. Learning sustainable results comes from inside yourself, by unlocking the power of your mind and your genius. All of those things that you reach out for externally—the things that you *think* will bring you happiness, love, wealth, and joy—will only bring you heartache, sweat, and tears. You can believe it or not: it doesn't really matter to me.

What should matter is what you want. Are you worth it? Are you willing to do what it takes to gain cohesive relationships, money, career, vacations, and an IRA that you will live off forever?

If you are not willing, then you're getting in life exactly what you have given. I know that I wanted more and that there had to be a way other than the path I was on. Unlock your mind, and the results will follow.

HORSES AND HUMANS

How does this show up in horses? What if I were to take you out in the arena, for example, and you had your vision and your focus at the right level? What if you knew what you wanted with compassion, love, and desire? You'd think this would serve you well, right? Let's say that every time you'd come in the past, you'd played with the same horse: Zeus. Over time, your relationship continued to improve and your communication became clearer when asking for jumps and sideways. However, today you're going to play with a new horse. His name is Script. Script is an old-timer. Your thought may be, *What could he show me? Why this horse?* Let's just use Script and be open to outcome, okay?

So okay, you play with Script and never before had you played with a horse that was so light, willing, and loving, yet dominant and clear. You play with all the same obstacles that you do with Zeus, and Script glides over and around with such beauty and connection that you're in a state of confusion. Is it him or me? Is it him showing me I can do this and these are my skills? Light, willing, loving, yet dominant and clear. Hmm, but with such beauty. Is that beauty in me? Of course I just didn't see it the same way Zeus had shown me.

With leaps and bounds, there is growth again. There is that moment when the feeling is like a tidal wave soaring you to the highest you ever imaged being in life. You never thought you could be there, but you are now. What a beautiful experience.

Every chance I get to spend with my horses, they show me something to help me be the best I can be. I love learning and, yes, it hurts sometimes. Remember that tears are healing. As with anything else, thinking without action is merely entertainment—at least, that's what Mary Morrissey says.[3] So even when it hurts, we can cry but we need an action step to move us forward. What are the results you want to create? Well then, dang it, go create it.

Essential Oils I would recommend:

The blend of essential oils found in **Hope™** brings an aroma that invites you to restore your faith by reconnecting with feelings of strength and stability.

---

[3] Speaker, best-selling author, and consultant for over four decades, Mary Morrissey's transformational talks and seminars have made her one of the elite teachers in personal development. As a sought-after expert on the "Spiritual Side of Success," Mary has spoken three times at the United Nations, facilitated three different week-long meetings with His Holiness The Dalai Lama, and met with Nelson Mandela in Cape Town, South Africa, to address the most significant issues our world is facing.

Sensation™ combines pure Ylang Ylang, Coriander, and other essential oils to encourage feelings of love and affection when diffused.

Transformation™ includes Idaho Blue Spruce, Palo Santo, and Ocotea. These powerful essential oils empower you to replace negative beliefs with uplifting thoughts when diffused.

Open to Outcome Activity:

What can I do in the direction of my dream today?

_____

_____

_____

_____

_____

What can I do in the direction of my dream to learn more?

_____

_____

_____

_____

_____

Who can help me in the direction of my dream?

_____

_____

_____

_____

_____

What do I have to let go of in order to create more results in the direction of my dream?

_____

_____

_____

_____

_____

What is it that I am so passionate about and why?

_____

_____

_____

_____

_____

Who can I share my dream with that will believe in me?

_____

_____

_____

_____

_____

What can I do in the direction of my dream to stay on track?

_____

_____

_____

_____

_____

What can I do with what I have to create _____? (You fill in the blank.)

_____

_____

_____

_____

_____

Chapter 8

Focus with Results

All blame is a waste of time. No matter how much fault you find with another, and regardless of how much you blame him, it will not change you.
—Wayne Dyer, co-author of *How to Get What You Really, Really, Really Want*

This is an amazing topic, and one I knew nothing about. For me, life just consisted of running around and constantly reaching for new things until something worked. **Literally**. Imagine something like the flying swing ride at the amusement park. I was every one of those legs, all flying in different directions at once.

The ability to focus is one that we need to learn. This all goes back to making it a point to think about what we really want in our personal and professional endeavors. Take the following five areas of life, for example, and determine what you really want, one measurable thing, for each of them.

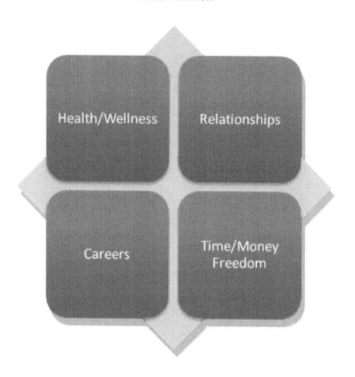

LONGING FOR MORE AS A STAY-HOME MOM

What are we looking for, and what should we be focused upon? Let me share a story, and I know many of you will relate to this one. A modern-day "wonder woman" at her best, Stacy is a stay-home mother with four kids. Her husband works full time, and sometimes even more than that. Although she worked full time in the pharmaceutical field before having children, Stacy is grateful for the opportunity to stay home with her children. There always comes a time, however, when despite the desire to be a big part of their child's life, a parent longs for something more. It just happens.

Life as a mother with four children is crazy busy from morning until night, with lunches, school, homework, dinner, laundry, sports, friends, and parties to plan and attend. It's very easy to forget about what she wants. That's because her focus, by default, is taking care of the kids. But why can't she do something nice for herself in the process? I'm not talking about getting her nails done, either—that's just an external factor that helps one feel good for a short time. It doesn't change how she will feel internally in the long run. What she wants, and we all want, is to feel important and valued, that she is more than a mother. She knows she is a woman, a daughter, a wife, a mother, and a child of God. Don't forget that. To feed her internal soul, she needs to change her self-image.

We cannot outperform what we cannot see. We know we want more, yet we don't often see a way out. Remember: the mind immediately starts asking "how" something can be done. It isn't possible to see all the answers to this "how," so we start with what we have and use that information to figure out where we want to go. That begins back in chapter one, Creating Results, and chapter two, It All Begins with a Vision.

PATTERNS AND HABITS THAT SHOW UP

It's so easy for you to *see* the day full of children. Your mind will picture what the day looks like without you even thinking about it. Life is made up of patterns and habits, and I want you to see that right here because so many people can relate to it. What is the pattern here? We've discussed this before: the subconscious mind need not think, but simply act. If we think, it is almost impossible to see anything else. It's embedded.

As a mother, you get up and are immediately on autopilot. You could walk and talk with your eyes closed, know which child is in bed, who isn't ready, and who is dilly-dallying in their room. Right? It's kind of like that old saying: "Mom has eyes on the back of her head." This is actually called intuition, and it happens when we're using our mental faculties along with understanding the patterns and habits that our children possess.

DESIGN VERSUS DEFAULT

Let's go back to Stacy for a moment. The question here becomes this: Is Stacy focusing on what she wants, or is she focusing on what she needs to do? Does she feel fulfilled? Everything starts in the mind. Harnessing success from within takes time, just like it took time to develop the patterns and habits she has now with four kids. She didn't just start them the second she had her first child. No, she created them by default, without even realizing it. This time, she must create them by design.

You'll never grow until you focus on what you want—you'll simply maintain the status quo. That focus comes with decisions. Everything you need comes from inside your consciousness. It's all there just waiting for you to tap into it. You might think that you don't know what to do, but at the center of everything your mind is clear and knows *exactly* what to do. All you have to do is choose to focus.

What you must do is form clear ideas of what you want, and this can be hard. When you're unsure about what you want and where you want to go, a great exercise is writing down a list of things that you definitely *don't* want. This is always easy to see first, and writing them down is a powerful tool. You can't just think this list, because it's impossible to figure everything out in your head, even if you really think you can. If you write it down, you're thinking *and* seeing your wants and needs. Most importantly, you're emptying your mind so that new information can help you find clarity. If you start this process by writing down things you definitely don't want, go ahead and reverse the statements:

I want less arguing.	I want to be more debt free.
I want more happiness.	I want less stress.
I want fewer bills.	I want more peace.

This is a great way to start creating and seeking what you want to do with your life. But first, remember that life is composed of habits and patters. Trying to instill a new habit can be really difficult. Take my book, for example: writing was not my specialty growing up. But I had a vision that I needed to share my story because so many people could relate to it. If I can do this, then so can other people, even if they doubt their ability. Can you relate to having made really poor life choices, then being so stressed that you almost had a nervous breakdown? How about having a heart catheterization ? Maybe you've dealt with an illness that almost took you down. Regardless, sometimes it takes this kind of shock to really discover your life's vision.

NAG ACTIVITIES

Exactly what am I telling you in this book? Well, I'm telling you that there's nothing you can't do. If you really want something, you can do it! It just takes focus and commitment to get there. It will take time, of course, and you'll have to stay focused to achieve your goal. But if you can do this faithfully, you can absolutely achieve your goal. What does doing something "faithfully" mean? For me, it means having a coach to work with who keeps me driving toward my dream. It takes blocking out time in my calendar to write, and then actually following through with those plans.

I had to change my lifestyle—my patterns and habits—to achieve my goal. One habit that I had to recognize was the fact that

I was always busy doing "safe" things. I was doing things that were easy, things that I was familiar with, and things that needed to be done. That did not include writing.

I call these safe activities "nag activities." These are activities that nag at you to take care of them until you finally give in. We know we have to do them, they take up space in our mind, and then we go do them. We might even feel like we're being productive in doing so; however, in reality, these are actually nothing more than interruptions in the progress towards our goal.

If something is important to you, you must focus and do what you need to do in order to be sure the outcome is what you want. So yes, I block out time to write. I make sure I'm in my office writing during those hours and that I'm doing what I need to for the outcome of producing this book. I also have to make sure others know how important this is and that interruptions are not an option.

Am I still focused on other things? Of course! Giving time for my family, my husband, and the different businesses I own, as well as giving time for me, are all very important to me. I'm especially fond of "me time" ☺. When I get me time, my writing flows easily and with less effort.

It's easy to get caught up in those "nag activities" and lose sight of what we really want. In order to overcome these activities, we have to change our habits. Creating new habits is much easier if we stay focused on the outcome. The outcome of this book is only the foundation for what's ultimately to come. Training modules, speaking events, workshops, and a million lives changing and growing. All of this is my ultimate goal, and all of this brings me much joy, peace, and success.

HORSE AND HUMAN

Last week in the arena, my client Kathy came to the realization that she wasn't focused on anything and that life around her was just happening on autopilot. Go here, do this, do that, stop this, move that, and so on. This was great awareness on her part, mind you, but it was a tough realization for her to swallow. She went about life doing everything but focusing. She didn't know what results she wanted or how to ask for them. Kathy couldn't envision what success would look like, therefore she had nothing upon which to focus.

I had Kathy complete an exercise with a horse called the "circling game." Think of your day as a clock: how do you use your time? What Kathy had to do was ask the horse to go out in a circle around her. She was on a twelve-foot rope/lead line. Once Kathy asked, her job was to do nothing. She needed to let the horse do what she asked of it.

First the horse did nothing. It didn't really even notice her. Just like a day in her house, with kids coming and going along with her husband—all the while Kathy just worked in the background, taking care of everyone and being available to solve whatever problem they were facing. Is there an emotion behind that action? Oh my gosh, yes! I'll tell you a secret: the emotion is FEAR. How does fear show up here? Think in terms of patterns and habits. It's possible that a lot of confrontation happened at home when Kathy was small, or maybe her parents were too busy to hear what she had to say and always silenced her. Maybe when she did speak up, others made fun of her. Life experience creates the results we see today. The result for Kathy was a lack of focus on what she wanted. Working with the horses allowed her to experience the possible outcomes and lean in and forward to get the results she wanted without verbal feedback, judgment, or feeling like a failure.

The second time around the circle, Kathy asked the horse with more energy. POW! The horse is bucking and kicking in a circle, and she doesn't know what to do. I tell her to breathe, and she does, so the horse settles. Completing the circle is akin to achieving the results you want to achieve in your life.

Kathy began to experiment with fear and what held her back. She leaned in and asked again. This time she got a few steps, a look of curiosity, and a "go ahead, make me." No, no, no! Never make me. Love me! So with a loving request, she asked again. The horse had a temper tantrum, anxiety kicked in, and Kathy panicked. She wanted to quit because that was easier. I encouraged her to stick with it for a few more minutes. I told her to breathe and clear her mind, and imagine how it would look and feel if the horse walked around her just one time. Baby steps! It would feel good, look pretty, and I would love it, is what Kathy said.

What just happened? Kathy became focused. She tried again with a more positive attitude, better clarity, and more direction. I'm sure you know what happened next. The horse walked the circle! She asked me if she could really apply this concept to her children and husband. Of course she could! The excitement she exhibited the following week assured me great things were happening. Kathy discovered that everything she wants, she doesn't get. The children finishing their homework before four, for example, or making sure the table is cleaned after dinner. She'd long since given up on asking for these kinds of things, as well as many others. Now that she knew the "secret"—that is, getting specific and being willing to ask for it—she could now focus on achieving the relationships and the life that she wanted with excitement.

INWARD SHIFT

When we seek "inward" for answers, the results are who we become in the process. Asking inward, Kathy thought about what would happen if she changed the way she asked. What was once "Please go take care of your homework" changed to "I want your homework done by four." Because she saw a vision, she knew the results she wanted to create. As a result, she got specific with her requests and took action. She loves the new person she is becoming, and everyone else loves the change. All of this happened because she was willing to look inward at her life and how *she* showed up.

Are things going to work the first run out? Mostly likely not, but if we keep leaning forward, more opportunities will show up to lead the way to where we are to be in life.

My son said to me the other day, "Do you know why most animals live short lives and why humans live so long? It's because humans don't know how to love." It takes us anywhere from sixty to eighty years to figure out how to love without judgment or expecting something in return. Wow! Focus inward, love every inch of yourself, and love will grow outwardly.

CREATING NEW HABITS

When you are creating new habits, the ones that you are deliberately making will take commitment, time, and persistence. It takes about twenty-one days to instill that new habit within yourself. So if you're looking to change your relationship with your spouse, for example, and increase communication, intimacy, and time together, then for twenty-one days I encourage you to try something new each day. The focus is not just bringing him coffee each morning. The focus is on love. What can you do to express love for him each day? Try this for twenty-one to thirty days and see how the relationship begins to evolve into something you've always wanted.

How about another example. Your career can be stressful, long, and frustrating. Are you focused on the good or the bad? This goes back to understanding that what you focus on is what dictates your results. What you think is what will happen. Everything is created twice. If you think it, then you bring it to life. If you are thinking about work being stressful, long, and frustrating, then how is that affecting you mentally (getting the results you think), physically (muscle tension and ache), and spiritually (negative begets negative)? This doesn't mean that the frustration isn't there; however, instead of focusing on it, think about what you can do to get positive results every day.

Take twenty-one days, and every night before going to sleep, write down all the good things that happened throughout the day. Then write down all the great things that will happen tomorrow. Before closing your eyes, imagine everything that you've written down harmoniously working out and the day running smoothly. Allow the mind to find the answers while you sleep.

DO YOU LOOK DOWN OR FORWARD?

When you are out taking a walk, do you find yourself looking up and forward or looking at the ground? Most people stare at the ground. Whether walking, driving, or riding a horse, staring at the ground will have the same effect. You don't get in your car and stare at the steering wheel, do you? No. You trust that the car will do what it's supposed to do as long as you look forward and drive. If you didn't look forward, where would you be going?

Everything we do has an inward and outward relationship. Outwardly, we are taking action. Inwardly, we have to trust that we can do it. When we come into alignment, great things happen.

HORSES AND HUMANS

If you're working with horses and look down, where do you think the horse will go? He might move forward, but it will be slowly or frantically because there is no alignment with what you're asking and where he is supposed to go. I love when we, as humans, demand and then blame others for the outcome. Is the horse dumb for not being able to magically sense where you want him to go? NO, it's always about the human.

If I've asked him to just walk with me, then my focus is to walk

111

the obstacle course, walk the outside walls of the arena, or go in a figure eight. It is his responsibility to stay with me. I look forward and start walking, and he will follow. If he lags behind, I may ask him again and he'll catch up. When I am focused and moving in the direction of what I want, there will be an alignment between me and the horse. When there is that alignment, I see the image internally and can easily ask for what I want, and what comes with that is harmony.

I refer to this as your POWER. When you focus, move forward, and trust what is happening internally, you will see it manifested externally as results—living in harmony and authentic alignment.

Get in harmony with some great oils:

Brain Power™ is a blend of essential oils high in sesquiterpenes— like Royal Hawaiian Sandalwood, Blue Cypress, and Frankincense— to promote a sense of clarity and focus when used aromatically.

Live with Passion™ fosters an optimistic attitude and general enthusiasm for life.

Combining essential oils chosen by D. Gary Young for their connections to our history, **Build Your Dream™** empowers and clarifies to help you find the way to achieve your dreams when used aromatically.

Focus Activity:

Where is it you need to get focused?

_____

_____

Why is this important to you?

_____

_____

How will you know you've accomplished what you're focusing on?

_____

_____

How will it make you feel when you're done?

_____

_____

How long will you give yourself to accomplish the object of your focus?

_____

_____

Who can help you along the way?

_____

_____

What will you feel like if you don't stick to your commitment?

_____

_____

Chapter 9

Perception

We come this way but once. We can either tiptoe through life and hope that we get to death without being too badly bruised, or we can live a full, complete life achieving our goals and realizing our wildest dreams.

—Bob Proctor

So many wonderful things are happening. Yet we are so challenged by decisions, obstacles, and thoughts—as well as culture and society—that sometimes our thoughts can lead to wanting to give up instead of persevering forward. Why is this? Well, there are many reasons. One important reason is that of our own perception. Perception is one of our six mental faculties, and we often do not realize how important it is. Many people know what perception is, but do we really know how it affects us? Perception is the ability to see, hear, or become aware of something through our senses. It is the **awareness** of something.

Maybe at this very moment you're thinking, "Hmm, what does she mean? The awareness of something. What am I supposed to be aware of?" You should be aware of everything and nothing. What I mean by this is you must be aware of what is most important, yet there are many things we do not need to be aware of and have no importance in our mind. One of the challenges you face in life is how you look at things. You've heard me say this before: how you do one thing is how you do everything.

THIS IS THE ONLY WAY

Connecting with so many people, I find it fascinating how one can look at things a single way. I bet you know someone like the "no" person. They are the eldest of the siblings, always having to take care of their younger ones. Remember, life is full of patterns and habits. These people are serious and their favorite word is no. "No" because: we are too busy, we have homework, mom would be mad, because I said so—just a whole lot of "because." They're truly just doing what they think mom and dad would, and in the process parents are instilling the value of "no" into their children. Being the eldest is a great responsibility that parents influence.

Now the child is grown, and what do you think happens? Their personality is serious, dry, and very simple. They now have children, and "no" comes right back to them. The interesting thing about all of this is that no one ever explicitly told them not to have fun, be adventurous, do things with imagination, etc. As life goes on, the idea formed in them that this is the way it is. It's the only way. Truly it's not, however, and what I really hear in my experience is that they *want* to say yes, but they are worried about what others will think. So they stay in their paradigm of comfort. Their perception is that this is the way life should be.

OPEN HOUSE AT THE RANCH

In actuality, there are so many ways to look at something. As a coach, it amazes me how one circumstance can be seen in so many different ways. I remember one of my first open houses at the ranch, when we had approximately thirty people attend. It was a glorious day. The sun was shining, so we did the open house outside on the playground. Yes, the playground that has toys in it for horses: a car wash, several jumps, a pedestal, and a see-saw, all on the lush green grass.

Our team took chairs out for everyone, and we horseshoed up for an opportunity to meet each other and have everyone introduce themselves with their name, where they're from, and what they thought we did. I chuckled as I heard some of their ideas about what we did! Of course, some people said that they had no idea what we did, and that's why they were there. Perception is awareness. I wanted to give them awareness about what I do.

During the open house, everyone participated in a session called "team penning." We broke the thirty people into five groups and asked them to pick a horse and bring them into their pen. We added a twist and said that they had five minutes to plan with their team, they couldn't touch the horse, and they had fifteen minutes to get the horse in its pen. Perceptions ran crazy. They all thought I was nuts. I wanted to just tell them what I did and have them experience it, too, because we are an experiential company that brings about awareness and reflection.

Five minutes of planning passed quickly, and it was time for the teams to move the horses. It's a pleasure to watch and learn, but it doesn't matter what I think. All that matters is what others are thinking. Now you can image how this was going. One team was staying in front of the horse, asking him to come forward, and in the mist of that one person in their group was off to the side with their own thoughts. Another group talked it out very well and all stood around the horse from shoulder to butt and back up the other side of his shoulder. No one stood in front. They used slapping sounds and smooches to encourage the horse forward and into his pen. You see where I'm going? After fifteen minutes had passed, we rounded up in the horseshoe, and I observed everyone coming back. Some were smiling and laughing, while others were frowning and mad. I wonder what happened out there?

Thirty people took their seats. We always allow a few minutes of talking because they're all excited to express their experience. The time rolled around to welcome everyone back to the circle, and we asked, "What happened out there?" The feedback was outstanding. Their perceptions ranged from having a really great team, to some being frustrated because others wanted to do things their way, to no one listening to them. I told them we needed to stand behind and not in front. Essentially, there were thirty different perceptions of what happened out there, but there was only one task. How is that possible?

It's possible because there is always a different way to look at something, do something, get something, etc. It's just a matter of whether or not we're looking at the different ways, thoughts, and expressions, or just thinking and doing what we want and know.

Take this image. What do you see?

Do you see lovely trees with rippling water and buildings behind it? Do you see a large face in the center? Maybe you see an old woman walking?

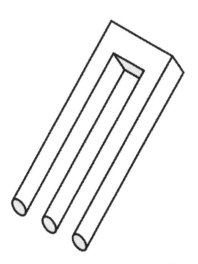

Are there three or four logs in this image?

Take a glass of water: is it half empty or half full? I once heard a story where a young boy was asked this question, and he answered that it was both.

Harnessing success from within means being able to openly take a look at ourselves and ask which we have: a growing mindset or a limited mindset.

LIMITED MINDSET

The limited mindset has one perception regarding how things are and how they've always been. A person with limited mindset gets up and does the same thing day in and day out, the same routine without fail. In fact, they will go to the same store, buy the same clothes, and any deviation away from this pattern in their eyes is wrong.

GROWING MINDSET

The growing mindset is one that is always seeking to try things a new way—a *different* way. These individuals look at the circumstance or situation and ask, "How can I do this quicker? How can we change direction and still get to where we're going? Can I do it with less effort and time but see more results?"

BREAK THROUGH

Life is what you make it. Yes, it is what it is. How can you grow from that to create the life you'd love? You can't get to where you are going without seeing it first. You're not going to have all the answers at once, nor will everything always work out just right along the way. Life is like a path of stones: the path is not so straight, and that's okay. That is, in fact, the journey—you keep taking steps on stones in a forward direction until you see what works and what doesn't. You ask, "How can I see this differently?"

What if someone told you there was gold on the other side of a wall? You couldn't see it, but you know it's there. Would you not keep walking forward? Of course you would. So then don't stop dreaming and imagining what it is you want. Keep taking steps forward, regardless of how hard it may seem. It's in those very moments when you really need to lean in and forward. Through the hard times, you grow the most and have what is known as "quantum leaps."

At this stage of the journey, you're looking for new ideas and ways to grow your dream. You're probably doing a lot of thinking. You have an image or vision, you've overcome some obstacles, and you've made important decisions. Now you need some breakthrough ideas. Here is where you begin to move closer to your vision.

HORSE AND HUMAN

How does this show up in our ground activities? You've heard the earlier story about my open house and others' perceptions, but let's take it down to one-on-one. Take that now-familiar activity of team penning. You've listened to what everyone else said; now consider it in relation to your life.

The self-awareness for one young lady, I recall, was this: "I was scared, so I didn't really participate and feel like I've let others down." Hmm … great awareness/perception. Let me ask, "Is it fact or truth? Did you go out, have conversations, walk, and stay with the group? Well, yes. So were you really scared? Did anyone say that you let them down? I think I heard the group say that there was great teamwork. The truth is that you did participate, you accomplished the task with your team, and everyone was quite pleased."

Where does this show up for you in life? What could you do differently? There are always different perceptions if you are open to seeing them. So often at a point when you feel stuck, you simply need to ask how you can change the perception to get back into the forward momentum of life. If it isn't working, take a different look at the circumstance or situation and shine the light of awareness on what you need to see, not just on what is showing up.

Oils that I recommend:

Containing Coriander and Geranium essential oils, **Acceptance**™ encourages feelings of self-worth when used aromatically.

Harmony™ is a blend of pure essential oils that contains scents to provide an uplifting aromatic experience.

Surrender™ is a blend of Lavender, Black Spruce, Roman Chamomile, and other essential oils that provides aromas to help cast off inhibitions that may be controlling your life or limiting your potential.

Perception Activity:

What can you do differently in life?

_____

_____

_____

Breaking through ideas for what you can do in the direction of your dream:

Idea # 1_____ Action Step_____

_____

_____

Idea # 2_____ Action Step_____

_____

_____

Idea # 3_____ Action Step_____

_____

_____

Idea # 4_____ Action Step_____

_____

_____

When will you do this by? Within one day, two days, or three. But no less. Ideas are powerful doors that just opened. Don't wait, don't think, just move in the direction and take the step. ☺

Chapter 10

The Frequency of Your Thoughts

Dreaming without action is merely entertainment.
—Mary Morrissey

Thinking is one of the hardest things we do—that's why most people just don't bother. They stop thinking and questioning and instead just accept whatever is easy. From the very start of the book, however, we talked about how important thinking and imagining are to our success. This is, admittedly, hard work. But as we climb the ladder of thinking, it gets easier and more powerful. Why is that? Well, the increasing power of our minds comes from the vibration or frequency we create when we think.

It took me a while to really understand and embrace this idea. It wasn't something I was ever aware of, and my mind seemed to actively resist the possibility of it being so. My thinking was so limited to only working a single way that the idea of there being something more behind the thinking process was almost unbelievable. The science behind the mind was not something about which I inquired, read, or studied. In fact, I thought it was all just a part of someone's crazy imagination. Did you hear that? I genuinely thought it was just someone's imagination that our minds could create a frequency. You know how TV can be with all the sci-fi stuff out there—who knows what to believe?

For me, the idea that our minds create a frequency really began to make sense once I started learning about horses and how to connect with them. It's understood that horses have a universal language and that anyone can understand them when we take the time. We have mouths where horses don't, but we both have frequency.

How do horses create a frequency? Their day typically consists of grazing, playing, resting, and using their mental faculty of alertness and intuition. They can sense far and near when danger is present. How is this possible? Well, I have an idea. It's the sensing of a thought generated by a desire that ignites an energy that radiates outwardly. The outward vibration is a frequency. That frequency is what saves their lives. I mean, there isn't anyone there to say, "Hey be careful—there is a bear nearby," you know? They have to go off of the frequencies around them.

GRAVITY

Some of you might be thinking, "How is that possible?" We don't have the answers to everything; sometimes we have to just trust that it is. We have to trust that, yes, we create a frequency. Take a look at gravity.

Gravity or **gravitation** is a natural phenomenon through which all things with energy are brought (or *gravitate*) toward one another. Consider for a moment how all things move. How does the ocean create waves? How does the air produce wind? We live in a universe of gravity. We can't explain everything, and yet we know it is so because it happens. The same is true of horses: we know it is so because it happens.

CREATING A FREQUENCY

How do humans create this frequency? You read that gravity is something brought towards you, yes? Like attracts like, so positive attracts positive and negative attracts negative. So far you're with me? Good. Take a moment and think about a couple that has been together for several years, and today they celebrate life. The celebration is a wedding, and it is taking place outside near the lake with beautiful green grass and simply placed white chairs with flowers all about. All of this generates and creates a beautiful fragrance in the air. You sit, witness, and begin to cry because it's so beautiful. What begins to happen to the people around you? Do others cry? Thinking generates feeling, which give you results—in this case, crying. When one cries, others cry. The frequency is a joyful cry.

Step into the celebration and food, the music and laughter. How does this make you feel? You feel great! You're happy for the newlyweds and you feel good. You feel so good that the night carries on until darkness falls, and because it feels so good you still don't want to leave. Hmm ...

Just consider all of life's experiences and how they make you feel. Let's take a look at some of the most commonly experienced emotional events.

- Baby being born
- Graduating

- Buying your first home
- Selling your first home
- Moving
- Getting married
- Losing a loved one
- Starting a new job

Whatever you think in that moment is the frequency you're attracting. Have you ever been in a crowd and seen someone you didn't want to talk to? Maybe you're standing there saying to yourself, *I hope she doesn't come this way, I hope she doesn't come this way* ... and what happens? She comes that way.

What I find most interesting is that people can generate a higher frequency of negative than positive outcomes. We can easily think about what we don't want and attract it. What would happen if you really embraced thinking about you do want, imagining what you would love, and began attracting that?

Consider for a moment what you're thinking and feeling. Would you say your current thoughts and emotions give you life? Do they make you feel excited, joyful, and happy? Notice how you feel in relation to the thought, "This feels great." You've just been told you won $20,000 dollars. What are you thinking right now as you're reading this? Write it down. Put words into vibrations of feeling. You want this and more where that came from.

Now consider for a moment that you're in a hurry; you're late for work and you will be fired if you are late one more time. You walk outside to the car and have not just one flat, but possibly two. Oh my! Do you notice what you're noticing? What is your first thought? Write it down right now, the thoughts you have about the flat tire. Now notice: how does it make you feel? Let's take this one step further. You go inside to call the mechanic to come save you and when you're done and go back outside, the possible other flat is, in fact, flat now. The rest of the day you complain, drop things, miss calls, and nothing goes right. Like attracts like.

How can you change? What if, instead of panicking or indulging in anger at the sight of the two flat tires, you generated a more productive thought: *Hmm, must be time to see the mechanic.* You call, he is happy to assist you, and is out in ten minutes with a quick fix—and just like that, you are on time for work. How would the rest of your day go? Do you think that this stuff just happens? Or do you accept that you could possibly be the cause of circumstances and results?

If you're not happy with life, want to change where you are, and wish to increase abundance and love, it's not outside of your reach. The means is inside of you.

How would or could your world change?

INCREASE ABUNDANCE WITH THINKING

How do your thoughts give you positive results in life? Are they holding you back from the power of living the life of which you dream? You have to consider how your thoughts impact the results you have in life. Sometimes, for instance, you do one thing but are really thinking another. Are you doing something for your husband or wife and then later mentally saying that she or he is a jerk? Is the person you work with extremely annoying, and yet you fake it to make it?

You can't do one thing, think something else, and then expect a positive outcome. It doesn't work that way. The results you get are specific to the thoughts you think. Refer back to chapters one, two, and three. In your thinking, you create a vision with your imagination and get specific. Now think about what you want.

The thinking creates a feeling, feeling creates results, and results create action.

If you're thinking positively, what frequency are you generating? What gravitational pull? Like a magnet, when and if we are in alignment with what we think and feel, then the action is to draw it to you. Attract it.

If you're thinking negatively, what frequency are you now generating? What gravitational pull? Are you getting what you want, or are you getting what you're thinking? Almost always, you're getting what you're thinking because this is what creates a feeling, which, in turn, generates the energy. High energy or low energy? Overly excited or sitting quietly?

This is way more simple than you think, so don't overanalyze it. Overthinking it will only end up with you stuck and frustrated. The problem isn't in anyone but you. Your results in your dream, circumstance, or life are not going to change until you do. It's not external; it's internal. It starts with your thinking.

HORSE AND HUMAN

This is easy. If we think that we won't get the horse to do something that we want, what happens? The mission is to walk into the pen and have the horse come to you. Your thoughts may be that *he will never come to me, he doesn't know me,* etc.

Steve comes for a session because he is feeling as if no one understands him. This is a great situation for a session. When others do not understand, neither will the horse. We ask him to go get one of the horses in the pasture because it's time for a session. He is excited, happy, and can't wait for a session. He also knows he only has an hour. His thinking on the way out to the pasture is that the horse will just come to the gate when he gets there. On the walk out his thoughts change to *he doesn't know me so he won't come. He probably will be afraid of me. He doesn't want to come in because it's too nice.*

What happens? He gets to the gate, he smooches and whistles, and yet the horse makes no movement. He goes into the pasture and starts walking towards the horse, and at first the horse doesn't move; but as he gets closer, the horse moves in the opposite direction. In fact, he runs away from Steve. Steve proceeds forward, and in doing so, he gets angry and frustrated.

Steve finally comes back to the gate and says, "I'm done with today's session. I see I have fifteen minutes left and I still don't have the horse." The following is the conversation that changed his perception and opened Steve up to the power of his thoughts.

Facilitator: What happened out there?

Steve: That horse doesn't like me.

Facilitator: What gives you that idea?

Steve: Didn't you notice? I couldn't get near him, and he kept running away from me.

Facilitator: I saw him moving around.

Steve: Really moving around. I am so frustrated. Didn't he know that I was just coming to get him?

Facilitator: I'm not sure, were you thinking about getting him?

Steve: Well, not exactly.

Facilitator: What happened?

Steve: I was so busy thinking he wouldn't come to me that he didn't understand what I wanted.

BIG QUESTION:

Facilitator: Where does this happen in your daily life?

Steve: Oh, wow. You're kidding.

Facilitator: Nope, not kidding. Where does this happen for you?

Steve: My kids; every time I want them to do something, they take off. Hmm.

Facilitator: I wonder why that is?

Steve: Well, isn't it obvious now? It's me.

Facilitator: Great observation and self-awareness. So, Steve, what can you do differently?

Steve: Really?

Facilitator: Do you want them to keep running, or do you want them doing what you ask?

Steve: What I ask. Okay. Well I need to think about what I want and then be sure to think of the results I want and express that clearly.

Facilitator: Excellent. Can you give me an example?

Steve: Yes. When it's bath time and everyone takes off doing something else, I am also thinking that the kids won't want to come in. So I will get excited about baths, ask them to come in because we don't want the house to smell, and bam!

Facilitator: Great job! Will you apply this when you get home?

Steve: Why wouldn't I?

Can you see this concept applied in your life? Can you see the importance of how you see things and what you are creating? I spent many years trying to change the people around me, chase after my dreams, and in the end, I only pushed them away. The power you need to create is within you, and you can attract it when YOU change you. You look inward at what it is you want and long for. Others will follow. I assure you; life becomes so amazing that it's hard to put into words.

Essential Oils I recommend:

Abundance™ combines oils such as Orange and Ginger, which were used by ancient cultures to attract prosperity and magnify joy and peace.

The **3 Wise Men™** blend contains Sandalwood, Frankincense, Myrrh, and other essential oils and is designed to promote feelings of reverence and spiritual awareness.

Envision™ contains scents that stimulate feelings of creativity and resourcefulness, encouraging renewed faith in the future and the strength necessary to achieve your dreams.

Change the Frequency Activity:

What is a goal or vision that you really want and are looking to accomplish?

_____

_____

What are the thoughts around that?

_____

_____

What feelings does this vision or goal generate?

_____

_____

Does it make you come alive? Or does it feel constricted?

_____

_____

If the feeling is constricting, you need to change this. Write down all the feelings you're having about what you would love. After writing them down, I want you to create a positive statement from that.

Ex:

No one will believe I can do it.	vs.	I only need to believe I can do it.
I don't have enough money.	vs.	Money is available to me.
I don't have a degree.	vs.	Many are practicing without the degree.

Every negative thought has a positive aspect. I don't care what the thought is. You just need to look at the positive side of it to create a frequency to attract the answers and what it is you want. Does the thought make you feel good? Stay with that frequency. Just like starting a new sport, job, or training, there are new muscles you need to form. Practice, practice, practice as frequently as necessary with persistence, and you will be rewarded immensely.

Chapter 11

Become a Magnet: Put on the Becoming

Everything you want is just outside your comfort zone.

—Robert Allen, co-author of *The One Minute Millionaire*

We have six mental faculties:

1. Imagination
2. Perception
3. Will
4. Intuition
5. Memory
6. Reason

Throughout the chapters of this book, we've been working on empowering all of them. I encourage you to master them. Mastering them creates the ability to bring forth the life that you seek. There are many thought leaders that understand the power behind mastering the mind: Napoleon Hill, Wallace Wattles, and Henry Ford are just a few.

This *becoming* is just like the other chapters: a stepping-stone to the love that we want. Have there been crossroads along the way? Of course! That is life. Today, and every day, is a new day. You can choose to allow the situations and circumstances to have you, or you can have them. We so often allow the circumstance to have us, and in doing so become victims.

Susie, one of my clients, has had many mortgages in her time. In fact, she has worked in real estate for many years and is quite good at it. She has bought and sold many properties and increased her wealth with her abilities in the process. She has achieved great accomplishments in life because of the wealth she has brought herself and her family. That wealth has given her gifts along the way, like a brand-new custom home, college for her children, and the freedom to live life at its fullest.

As life continued to evolve, Susie had to do some restructuring in order to take it to the next level. This meant obtaining a mortgage of significance. In order to accomplish that, she had to leverage her personal home to gain another level in life. However, in doing so, a new pattern resonated. That pattern was self-worry about the loan and how much it was. Interestingly enough, she had many loans that totaled more than this one, but because the mortgage loan in question was personal, it really grabbed ahold of her life.

Susie would talk about the loan with increased bass in her

voice, so much so that her voice would increase in volume and speed as well. Her thoughts revolving around the loan were ultimately diminishing and controlling her. She needed to figure out a new way to get the loan paid off. Her thoughts carried on and on with how, how, how, how. It was making her sick. Let me ask you: Did this circumstance have her, or did she have the circumstance? It had her. When we allow our circumstances to have us, our energy and vibration within begin to diminish. She had to do something fast.

To *put on the becoming* means stepping into every part of who you are and staying there, even when times feel challenging. Her becoming was a successful entrepreneur, and all of a sudden, she allowed something to take that away from her. So we went back, rewrote, and generated a new thought of becoming.

To become, we must will it. We must have this burning desire of something we want and be able to see it. It's taken me some time to get to this point and to realize that, yes, we have the ability within us but we cannot do it alone. We must have God in our life. God created and knows everything about us. It is us that has to discover us. You see, we use a phrase of words so often and do not see how they affect our circumstance. This is the power behind the words "I am." God didn't put us on earth to say, "I am not." He said, "I am that I am." Now every single time you say the words "I am," you are citing the name of God. We need God in every area of our lives. He is the universe. He is the infinite. He is the magnetic force behind all creation. When you say that you are sick or unlucky, what you are really doing is desecrating and disrespecting the name of God. Who wouldn't want God on their side, regardless of what has happened in life? We may not always agree with or understand why he acts as he does, but no matter what, I always want him near me and not my enemy.

In the becoming we use and call forth the power of "I am." I am a growing, loving child of God. I am lucky. I am healthy. There is power in words. Going back to Susie, she changed her thoughts in support of who she really was, and said it so well that she was able to recall her focus. Her thoughts used to sound like, *This is the biggest mortgage I've ever had. I have to get it paid, I have to, I have to, I have to,* even though she has had mortgages throughout her life that totaled more than what she financed. In addition, she has equity in all her investments and could have easily paid off her debt. However, her limited thinking took over, and we had to change that. In changing her thinking, what she now said was, "I am able to make good decisions. I refuse to focus on what I don't want. I've had mortgages and paid off mortgages. I've done this again and again, and I'm doing it now." That is exactly what she has done. Do you see and feel the differences between those two thoughts?

You must see your dream of being. You want to be that author. How would an author act? What would they be doing every day? If you want to become a yoga expert, then what would they do with their daily lives? In the beginning, the answer might be something as small as watching a free how-to video. But above all, it involves imagining. "I am" an author. "I am" a yoga instructor. "I am" a financial advisor. With this imagining, you will succeed.

Becoming is the knowing and seeing what it is we want and acting in that manner. If I want to be a successful chef who owns a multi-million dollar restaurant, would I go home and eat boxed frozen food? Would I be sitting with friends that complain all the time? Of course not. I would find friends that want to better themselves and learn about running a successful restaurant. I would probably eat dinner at the restaurant before I went home. I would act as if I have it already, do what I can do with what I had, and expect that more will follow.

HORSES AND HUMANS

Horses can easily sense our incongruences. So often who we think we are and how we show up are two different beings in one. We begin with an activity of self-awareness. Who do we think we are, and how does that differ from how we act?

The sun is shining early, the horses are all playful this morning, and Michelle comes for her session. During this session I give a Michelle a piece of paper, and on that paper are characteristics, words that describe how one feels and acts. Her job this morning is to identify three horses and their characteristics. Now remember the horses act as a mirror directly to our souls.

After about twenty minutes of observation, we take the activity back to the classroom. Michelle identifies all the characteristics. One horse might be smart, playful, naughty, and exuberant. Horse number two might be bold, pushy, and demanding. The third horse is clumsy, lazy, and forgiving. Excellent. I ask, "Does any of this sound familiar?"

With that exuberant energy, Michelle says, "Yes, horse number one is me."

Great! "How are you playful, naughty, and exuberant?" I ask her.

"Well, hmm, when I am in public," she responds.

"Oh, okay. Is there something else you'd like to share?"

"Yes, I am really horse number three," she confesses.

"Oh, really?" I ask. "Tell me more."

"When I'm home, I don't clean my house or do things I should, and yet when I'm out I appear to have it all together and get silly and have fun because I want people to like me."

"Oh. How is that working out?"

"Not so good," she responds.

"Maybe you'd like to try something new," I offer.

"You know, I think I should."

"Great. What will you do?"

"I would much rather get fun and silly at home, too, and get things done. It would make me feel good." Bingo.

We came up with a schedule that Michelle can work with to reach some goals.

Was Michelle aware that this incongruence existed? She had NO idea. It was a powerful session and great results came of it. I remember her husband coming to observe a session because he wanted to know what I was doing to his wife that was making all of these changes. I laughed, and love when this happens, because it isn't me at all. It's the power in the person to see through new eyes who they are and grow from the inside out.

Maybe you're reading this and it is resonating with you. Michelle wasn't aware. Many others come to the facility and are aware. They can tell me, "Yes I know." Yet what comes next is this confession: "But I guess I really didn't know." We think we know; but we really don't understand what that means UNTIL we experience something that shines the light of awareness on it and we finally SEE it.

A young man, Paul, knew he was impatient and would rather do things than wait for someone else to do it. He knew this wasn't nice, and caused him to stress about it, yet nothing ever stopped him or changed how he handled things UNTIL the light of awareness shone bright. Paul's personal experience in the arena was heart wrenching. He knew. He thought he knew. Now he knows. He felt horrible to be taking away from others, stepping on them, hurting their feelings, as if they weren't good enough. Since that day of knowing, he now waits. Granted, when there is such a HIGH frequency, it takes time and practice to recondition our actions, but now that Paul is fully aware of his actions, he consciously works on improving that area of his life. He knows when he does this, he has less stress and more happiness.

Great oils I recommend:

Believe™ contains Idaho Blue Spruce, Idaho Balsam Fir, Frankincense, and other essential oils that may encourage feelings of strength and faith when used aromatically.

Live Your Passion™ essential oils to help you pursue life with greater purpose and attention on the endeavors that matter most.

Gathering™ features a blend of aromas that invite you to overcome the chaotic energy of everyday life and keep you on the path to higher achievement.

Becoming Activity:

Who do you want to become?

_____

_____

What would this person be doing?

_____

_____

Who would they surround themselves with?

_____

_____

How would they dress?

_____

_____

Where would they spend their time?

_____

_____

Create your "I am" statement, and begin it like this: "I am so happy and grateful now that_____."

_____

_____

Chapter 12

Gratitude and Support

Each and every chapter in this book has built upon the former; and now, at the very last chapter, we arrive at the concept of gratitude and support. As I write this, I also think about reciprocity. These are all important topics to cover, and they are quite possibly the most rewarding, yet the hardest, commitments to undertake. We often struggle with perception and forgiveness. In fact, we are often only willing to see things our way. We would rather hold onto resentment and anger than let it go, learn, and love. We let pride and ego take over instead of caring and compassion.

PRIDE AND EGO

You can hold onto all of your negative patterns and habits right along with ego and pride, but rest assured that you are not getting out of life that which you really deserve. The awareness of what you've heard me refer to as "limiting thinking" results in a limited lifestyle—and yet we swear by it. We push away people and opportunity instead of inviting them in. Look here:

The noun *pride* describes a feeling of happiness that comes from achieving something. When you do a good job or finish a difficult task, you feel *pride*. *Pride* can also have a negative meaning and refer to exceedingly high self-regard (Dictionary.com).

Your *ego* is your conscious mind, the part of your identity that you consider your "self." If you say someone has "a big *ego*," then you are saying he is too full of himself (Dictionary.com).

CONQUERING YOU

Conquering the success of knowing who you are is in all of these chapters. Every chapter discusses the importance of knowing of who you are (on the inside), how you show up (how you act in society), and your thinking patterns. It's important that you're focusing on *you* rather than a *thing,* because what you want in this world is not tangible. There is nothing tangible that will ever fully satisfy you. Every one of those tangible things—including your spouse, your car, your vacations, and friends—are all temporary.

Everything we really want in this life is peace, happiness, and love. Each and every one of us in this universe seeks and longs for these three things in life. Where we find them is not outside ourselves; it is inside the mind. This is the knowing that we can be who we'd love to be, act and do what we wish to do. We are perfectly okay to be ourselves—not what others expect and want and not what society demands of us in order to fit in.

When you can be you, there is peace, happiness, and love.

Each chapter takes you on a journey into creating what you want, living the life you love, and loving who you are. Life is short. Time is invisible. It continues to move forward day in and day out. Knowing this will alter your life in ways you can only imagine. Creating a life and following these principles creates new mental muscles. And just like muscles in other parts of your body, you have to continue to work on them to develop what it is you want. There will be times when you will want to fall back into old habits and patterns because it is comfortable and easy, but I assure you that once you've focused forward, you will not want to stay there long. The rewards are so magnificent that they will pull you forward on your journey. Whatever you're thinking, there is always way more. Way, way more.

ULTIMATE LIFE

Just imagine the ultimate life. I know exactly what you're thinking, as do so many others who start on this journey—and that is that it's "impossible." The only thing that is impossible is you. It's your thinking and lack of creative imagination that is limiting your life and your potential. If you want to get somewhere, you have to first think it. I know you're probably saying right now, "When, then how?" Great question. The mind does not answer these questions. They are unspecific, and the concepts too large to see every step from here to there. It's like asking your computer to do everything you want it to, but you don't know what you want exactly. What will you get from that? Not a whole lot. Begin with chapter one: imagine, dream about what you would love. Ask yourself, "What CAN I do with what I have in the direction of my dream?" The next step will show up, then the next—and then you can take bigger steps. Before you know it, the universe is pulling you forward to a life you imagined. How would that feel? It is powerful and enlightening, and you will want more.

If you want this life, you must leave negative patterns and habits behind. Anyone can do this with the right kind of support. How are famous people successful? How do you become an entrepreneur? How do you overcome a weakness? How do you become wealthy in love? If you go out and interview just those people, I will assure you that they didn't do it alone. There was someone there for them in the form of a program, coach, mentor, teacher, or friend.

RESOLUTIONS

Have you ever made a New Year's resolution and accomplished it?

U.S. World News states that 80 percent of people fail at completing their resolutions. Here is what they say.

To answer this question, it's important to recognize that outside-in solutions such as dieting, joining gyms, and so on are doomed to fail if, other than your well-intentioned resolve to change, you've done nothing to enhance your capacity to either sustain motivation or handle the inevitable stress and discomfort involved in change. Saying this differently: Unless you first change your **mind**, don't expect your health goals to materialize. As the saying goes, it's not the horse that draws the cart, it's the oats. It's not the gym, Pilates class, or diet that will change you—it's your mind.[4]

There are thousands of articles that support this assertion with science and thorough research. Henry Ford said, "If you think you can or you think you can't, you're right." So if you imagine a better life, yet think those self-sabotaging thoughts, then you won't accomplish anything. Are you getting how this works?

People who are successful in love, relationships,

---

[4] http://health.usnews.com/health-news/blogs/eat-run/articles/2015-12-29/why-80-percent-of-new-years-resolutions-fail

entrepreneurship, health, and finances put themselves out there and devote the time needed to achieve their goals, regardless of their life circumstances. There is determination (burning desire for more), focus, and persistence in what they want. The more you focus, the more you fine-tune. The more you do what you want and tune it up, the more you get.

GRATITUDE AND RECIPROCITY

We also have to be people of gratitude and reciprocity. This is another of those thinking patterns we forget to do and fall out of habit. Gratitude is the inner feeling of thankfulness. I know myself: I fell away from this. Not that I wasn't thankful, but grateful is at a much higher level. The awareness of gratefulness comes from love and compassion. Thankful is thankful. Grateful comes from seeing the good in everyone and in all circumstances:

1. Gratefulness for the young lady that checked you out at the supermarket, mind you, who wasn't very nice.
2. Gratefulness for the customer service representative on the other end of the line who wasn't very helpful.

It is from our gratefulness that we realize they are doing their best at the moment. You were there once, and you never ever know what is going on in that person's life that is causing them to react or behave in a certain manner. When you have gratitude, it sends love to wherever you are and reaches those individuals wherever they are in their lives. How can you be sincere in giving to someone who you may feel, at first, is undeserving? Give more. Make a conscious effort.

Go back to *like attracts like*. If someone isn't giving you the

153

help you want over the phone or in the supermarket, and you allow their attitude to affect you, what happens to you and why did you let that happen? You know, you walk out of the store or hang up the phone and you are so ticked off and irritated. The whole day gets worse and worse.

No, stop and rise above it. Have compassion and be grateful. If you can do these two things, then what are you doing for the aforementioned individuals? You are giving them the gift of reciprocity. Instead of you being the person attracting what you don't want, you can help those who also need to rise above, be an example, and pull them up. The feeling you feel afterward attracts more of what you want.

When I first started practicing these laws and others were having compassion and gratefulness towards me, I would just cry. The pouring, showing, flooding waters of love would overwhelm my emotions, and it would make me feel so good. It pulled me forward and lifted me up to heights I didn't know existed. Those are heights I now live at, want to stay at, and look to go higher. Just imagine.

HELPING VERSUS GIFTING

Some give and give and give, and that's great. I wonder if they see, however, that there is a time and place for how to give. I was a giver. I gave to my family, I supported them, I went over and above and my children will even tell you, I've given too much. In doing so, I enabled them. This was not good. Giving and helping is much different, and it's important to know these boundaries. Helping someone could be giving a hand. Helping someone may be meeting up and doing something together. Helping may be lending an ear.

Helping by continually bailing them out, on the other hand—by helping to pay a bill over and over, for example—is not the right way to go about things. I know it helps us, meaning the giver feels good, but this is one of those times when we are doing more damage than good. We are enabling this person instead of lifting them up. We are the cause of a pattern and habit that is not good, and it doesn't help them to grow.

This was a hard lesson for me. Part of this is because we try so hard to have people like us. Family and friends. You don't want to be alone, you want them to want to be with you, love you, and spend time with you. When you learn to be with yourself, get to know yourself, and love yourself, you will attract those healthy relationships. When you're the giver, it's one of the temporary fixes. It makes you feel good, but the results are not at all what you want.

Loving yourself is the hardest. Many, many people I have worked with and know personally are so critical and judgmental of who they are and what they look like. How can we love others if we cannot love ourselves? When you hear me speak about incongruence, this is one. Love yourself first. A book I so often refer to and share with many people is Louise Hay's *You Can Heal Your Life*. Again, this requires an inward shift that gives lasting outward results.

Gifting is a sign of appreciation. That can come in the form of helping, being there, lending a hand, etc.—it doesn't need to be something material. You can also give the gift of life. What comes to mind first is when someone has gone the extra mile for you, you can send a special note. Find out what they love most and give them a gift in that area. The best gift you can give is not what *you* want, but what *they* want, love, or need.

In business, you may give a gift as a reminder of how far a coworker has come. In personal development, we may give a journal to help stay on track or a bracelet as a reminder to keep dreaming and leaning into life. In real estate, maybe you'd give a welcome basket to a new tenant or a picture of the family in front of their new home. What does this hold? Happiness and joy. It reflects where they are, not what you want to give or what is easiest.

When we have gratitude and get support, life is on a pull of becoming, a pull of spiraling up and forward. The rewards significantly outweigh the dollars and time you put into receiving them. I feel I may have struck a note, and you just felt some tension about that. Hear me. You are not buying support. You are not buying gratitude. Let me be clear on this. You are investing in you. If you buy a building, you gain an income or rate of return. There is something to be said for this. It's growing, yes. Without that investment, would you grow in this area? Of course not. Maybe in another, like a stock.

Consider yourself a piece of real estate if you must. You will get NOTHING if you don't take the risk, make the commitment, and lean in with action. It is at that moment of commitment that the increase starts. How much are you worth investing in? Did I strike another nerve? I hope I did. You're worth the investment, whatever the cost might be.

Take, for example, working with a life coach. The coaching program could range from $500–$50,000 depending on who is going to be your life coach. Let's use a $500 investment for a seven-week program as our example. You tune in and turn up participation and, from that, you have more confidence and assertiveness. This means that your family is working with you, they are willing to stop and listen with you, and you've spoken up to your boss about issues you were having and how you could be more effective for him—and you got a raise. Would that be worth the $500 initial investment?

We usually want to see the results before we will invest. It doesn't work that way. This is about you. It's you who must make the commitment. The work is being done in you. The people around you are not going to fix the lack of communication or respect in your family—you need to do that. Your boss most likely is not going to come to you and say, "Hey, all your work is incomplete or not on time, so let me give you a raise." What has to change? You. What happens when you have to change? It's hard. Stretching and growing, however, will give you the greatest rate of return.

I ask you now, what would you rather do: keep complaining about life or do something about it? I know that from within you, there is peace and love and no matter what happens, you can do it. You can have anything you want, and it starts with investing time and effort in yourself. Imagine, dream, think of what you would love. Get a journal and start writing your thoughts down. Take a step, any step, but take a step forward and enjoy the journey.

HORSE AND HUMAN

This is a beautiful thing. Over time working with the horses, the lessons we learn are remarkable. The horses are so forgiving and hold no grudges or resentment, which is something all humans need to learn. In the beginning, it will also look imperfect. The good thing is that it will never look as bad as it does when we first start. This is how it is with anything. Think about the first time you played a sport or did yoga. *Oh my, don't look at me!* Over time and practice, we begin to master it. Same thing goes here. In fact, one of my mentors, Mary Morrissey and her team, always talk about "MASSIVELY IMPERFECT." Play all out. Dig deep and play hard.

Those lessons we learn in our growing phase—when they are massively imperfect—serve to build a relationship. In the arena, this relationship is between the horse and you. In life, this relationship is between you and everyone else. As those relationships grow, you love them, gain patience, and learn to ask lots of questions. When you do this in the arena, the horse is more eager to play it all out, be totally present, and give. In life, that is working in harmony with congruence. The remarkable feeling outweighs anything you could imagine. Start imagining and living life the way you want, true to who you are, and see the light shine on you. There isn't anything else in the world more valuable than that.

Oils I recommend:

Foster a grateful attitude and embrace the blessings in your life. The uplifting aroma of **Gratitude**™ invites a feeling of emotional and spiritual progress.

When diffused, **Present Time**™ helps you focus on the here and now, so you can get beyond the past and move forward.

Highest Potential™ harnesses the uplifting and inspiring power of Blue Cypress and other pure essential oil scents.

Horses love each and every one of the oils and then some. My guys are especially fond of Peppermint, Valor, Frankincense and my Animal Scents Ointment.

DREAM BIG! THINK BIG!
ASK BIG QUESTIONS AND GET BIG ANSWERS!

Where do you go from here? In my appreciation for you investing in yourself and taking the time to read my new book, I want to offer a complimentary guide, **7 Steps to Creating Your Life**. No matter where you are, no matter what you've done, or what's been done to you, no matter how bad things are, let's get started right here and right now.

COMPLIMENTARY GIFT

7 Steps to Creating Your Life

A guide to get you started creating the life you'd love. It walks you through the four quads of life—Relationships, Health, Career, and Time/Money Freedom—what you would love, and what action steps you need to take to get you moving in the direction of what is most important to you.

Go to www.yarcorteacres.com

Find the link: 7 Steps to Creating Your Life.

I can't wait to hear from you about how I can serve you.

About the Author

GINA YARRISH spent 30 years in Real Estate before finding her passion in teaching and coaching with horses. She offers a variety of development programs in life skills and leadership for youth, as well as personal and professional development for adults and organizations. Gina brings all her talents to her book to help you find your Purpose, Power and Peace.

References

Equine Experiential Education Association (E3A). E3A is an international professional membership organization offering training, certification and resources for the implementation of Equine Assisted Learning (EAL) programs by educators, coaches, Professional Development trainers and other facilitators. www.E3Assoc.org

Equine Assisted Growing and Learning Association (EAGALA). An association for professionals incorporating horses to address mental health and personal development needs? www.eagala.org

Jack Canfield. Principles of Success, page 6-7. As an internationally recognized leader in peak performance strategies, Jack delivers his innovative, unique and powerful success principles to enthusiastic audiences around the globe. Industries from Healthcare, fortune 500 companies, manufacturing direct sales, real estate, higher education and many more have been inspired and empowered by Jack's powerful message. www.jackcanfield.com

Mary Morrissey. World-renowned life coach, motivational speaker, spiritual author and the Founder of Life Mastery Institute. Author of two best-selling books, *No Less Than Greatness* and *Building Your Field of Dreams*, which became a PBS special. She's also been featured in The Moses Code, Beyond The Secret and several other popular films.www.marymorrissey.com

Parelli Natural Horsemanship. Parelli Natural Horsemanship's goal is to help raise the level of horsemanship worldwide for the benefit of horses and the people who love them. www.parelli.com

Steve Harrison Quantum Leap Program. A copywriter, creative director and author who is regarded by Campaign Magazine as the greatest Direct Marketing Creative of his generation. He has won more <u>Cannes Lions</u> awards than any other Creative Director in the World. <u>www.steveharrison.com</u>

Young Living Essential Oils. Through Gary and Mary's Young combined leadership, Young Living has grown to become the world leader in essential oils and wellness solutions. <u>www.youngiving.com</u>

Continue Your New Adventure With Gina

What's the next step?

Some of you know how valuable this information is and already want to go deeper. Don't stop here. The rewards are huge.

- If you want to join a program, need coaching or have an interest in connecting with Gina personally she can be contacted at gina.yarrish@yarcorteacres.com.

- For more about Gina Yarrish, visit www.yarcorteacres.com

Coming in 2017

- "Empower Thinking"– Thinking is the hardest thing we have to do and like exercising, it's a new muscle we must develop. Developing this muscle with Gina and jump start your coming year.

- Harness Your 3P's"- Surprise

- Harness Your 3P's - Retreat

Made in the USA
San Bernardino, CA
28 October 2016